ADDRESSES TO YOUNG MEN

ADDRESSES TO YOUNG MEN

Awakening Sermons for Slumbering Sinners

REV. DANIEL BAKER

PREFACE BY D.L. MOODY

SOLID GROUND CHRISTIAN BOOKS

BIRMINGHAM, ALABAMA USA

Solid Ground Christian Books
715 Oak Grove Rd
Birmingham, AL 35209
205-443-0311
sgcb@charter.net
http://solid-ground-books.com

ADDRESSES TO YOUNG MEN

Daniel Baker (1791-1857)

Taken from edition printed by Morgan & Scott, London

Solid Ground Classic Reprints

First printing of new edition February 2007

Cover work by Borgo Design, Tuscaloosa, AL
Contact them at borgogirl@bellsouth.net

ISBN: 1-59925-094-2

PREFACE BY MR. D. L. MOODY.

———◆———

I HAVE been frequently requested to publish my addresses, with a view of reaching, by this means, many more than those who hear them delivered. But on account of the very little time I can get for study, and the number of meetings at which I must be present, I have hitherto been unable to accomplish this. In reading two volumes of sermons, however, by the Rev. Daniel Baker, of America, preached thirty years ago, I have thought no addresses could be more suitable for the present times than these. They have been a great help to me; and many who are now preaching the gospel in America bear similar testimony. Knowing particularly that he was the *young man's preacher,*

I believe his printed sermons will give a fresh impulse for work to many, and be the means of pointing the way to multitudes who are inquiring.

May God, who alone can draw men unto Him, so use these words, that the writer of them, being dead, may yet speak with power to men's souls.

D L Moody

AUTHOR'S PREFACE.

———•———

THESE discourses were designed to be of an *awakening* character, and were preached (in substance) in numerous revivals, and were blessed to the hopeful conversion of many precious souls, of whom some fifty or more have become ministers of the gospel.

May HE who was pleased to bless these discourses when they came from the Pulpit, bless them also now coming from the Press. And to His great Name be all the praise!

CONTENTS.

———◆———

ADDRESSES TO YOUNG MEN.

TRUTH AND EXCELLENCE OF THE CHRISTIAN RELIGION.

"Their rock is not as our Rock, even our enemies themselves being judges."—DEUT. xxxii. 31.

THESE words form a part of what is usually denominated "the Song of Moses." It is a poem of singular beauty; and, by the best judges, is supposed to contain a specimen of almost every species of excellence in composition. It opens with a sublime invocation of the heavens and the earth; evidently designed to convey a strong idea of the peculiar importance of the subject matter of the poem.

The sacred writer speaks sublimely of Israel's God: "Ascribe ye greatness unto our God," says he. "He is the Rock, his work is perfect; for all his ways are judgment: a God of truth and without iniquity, just and right is He."

The author of the poem then adverts to some

I

instances of God's providential care exercised over the tribes of Israel, particularly in conducting them, as on the wings of an eagle, towards the promised land. "As an eagle," says he, "stirreth up her nest, fluttereth over her young, spreadeth abroad her wings, taketh them, beareth them on her wings; so the Lord alone did lead him, and there was no strange god with him." This idea of the tribes of Israel being conducted out of Egypt, towards the promised land, as upon the wings of an eagle, is one of great sublimity, particularly taken in connection with these words —"I kill, and I make alive; I wound, and I heal; neither is there any that can deliver out of my hand. For I lift up my hand to heaven, and say, I live for ever."

In comparison with such a God, the idol gods of the heathen were, emphatically, "vanity and a lie." No wonder, then, that Moses here indulges in the feelings of joy and triumph; no wonder that he uses the exulting language of our text: "Their rock is not as our Rock, even our enemies themselves being judges." Mark the expression— *Even our enemies themselves being judges.* Moses adverts, it seems, to some well-known instances, in which the superiority of Israel's God was acknowledged, even by those who served other gods, which indeed were no gods. This acknowledgment, it will be recollected, was made by the magicians of Egypt, when, utterly unable to resist the miracles wrought by Moses, the servant of the true God, they exclaimed, " This is the finger of God ! "—that is, this miracle comes from the true God. This acknowledgment was also made by the horsemen of Pharaoh, when, terror-stricken in the Red Sea, they cried out one to another, saying, " Let us flee from the face of Israel, for their God fighteth for them against the Egyptians." It was, it seems, in reference to these, and similar cases, that Moses used the exulting language of our text : " Their rock is not as our Rock, even our enemies themselves being judges."

And now, my brethren, permit me to apply the passage before us to a class of persons not entirely dissimilar. I mean to those ranged under the banner of Infidelity. Rejecting the sacred volume, they have a system of their own, if system it may be called. Now, in reference to them, and their system, I feel very free to apply the language of our text : " Their rock is not as our Rock, even our enemies themselves being judges."

It may be thought by some present, that the speaker is not happy in the selection of his subject this day, as there is, perhaps, not an avowed infidel in this assembly. But, suppose there be not an avowed infidel present, there may be many spiced with infidelity ; and amongst them, perhap s some interesting young men, who, in their reading and travels, have had infidel cavils and objections brought before their minds which they know not how to meet; the result is, they have become sceptical. This they are not exactly willing to confess, lest, perchance, it might reach a mother's ear, and pain a mother's heart!—but, the seeds of infidelity are there; and, so long as they exist in the bosom, they operate as serious barriers in the way of the soul's salvation. This being the case, it is proper that, occasionally, at least, the evidences of our holy religion should be laid before every congregation.

Those ranged under the banners of Infidelity may plume themselves upon their wisdom, and the great superiority of their discoveries, but, thank God, we, who are Christians, occupy better ground than they do; and may well say, with Moses, in the joy and triumph of our hearts—" Their rock is not as our Rock, even our enemies themselves being judges."

The supreme excellence and great superiority of the Christian religion will appear, I think, very clearly, in the three following particulars :—

   I. In the matter of evidence.

   II. In reference to the moral influence; and

III. In relation to the happiness of man.

   I. In the matter of evidence. Yes, my brethren, whatever witlings and infidels may say to the contrary, it is a stubborn fact, that this blessed volume called the Bible, comes to us with credentials clear !

> " On every line
> Marked with the seal of high divinity ;
> On every leaf bedewed with drops
> Of love divine, and with the eternal heraldry
> And signature of God Almighty stamped
> From first to last."

Yet the infidel rejects the sacred volume ! And why ? Oh, because he is a very reasonable man, and cannot, forsooth, without a prostration of everything like reason, embrace a system so preposterous and absurd ! Now let sound reasonings and facts be submitted to this enlightened and candid assembly.

1. If there be no Divine relation, as infidels are wont to affirm, herein is a marvellous thing, that there should be none ! And why ? For many reasons. One is this : There are certain questions propounded by human nature itself, weighty and important questions, and which, in the very nature of the case, never can be answered without a Divine revelation. For example : Where is God, my Maker ? The author of my being, who is he ? and what is he ? It will be recollected that this question was asked by Dionysius, the tyrant of Syracuse, to Simonides, one of the

seven wise men of Greece. The philosopher requested one day to think upon the subject; at the expiration of that period he demanded two days, and then four—doubling the time. When asked why he demanded so much time, he replied, " Sire, the longer I think upon this subject, the more I am lost in its difficulty and immensity."

In the very nature of the case, it is none but God that can reveal God; and yet the infidel scouts the idea of the Scriptures having been divinely inspired—and he, a reasonable man !

But another question propounded by human nature, is this: How can a man be just with God ? How can a man, who is a sinner, obtain the forgiveness of his sins, and be restored to the favour of his Maker ? This, my brethren, believe me, has for ages and ages been one of the most confounding and perplexing questions ever presented to the mind of man. Heathen sages, and some of the wise ones of the earth at the present day, talk about penances and pilgrimages, bloody sacrifices, costly offerings, repentance and reformation, and many such like things. But it is all conjecture; and, in a matter of such immense importance, I want something better than conjecture. I am a sinner. I feel it, and, troubled on account of my sins, I ask, with trepidation—How can a man be just with God ? How can I, a poor burdened sinner, obtain the forgiveness of my sin, and be restored to the favour of my God? I listen, and there is no response! There can be none, save from the throne of God!—and, without it, I live in darkness; I die in gloom, and, sinking in the cold embrace of death, I have only to say with the dying Adrian, " Alas! my trembling, dear, departing soul, whither art thou going ? "

I say there can be no response, to satisfy the troubled conscience, save from the throne of God. The case is clear. Take this illustration. I have injured you: upon reflection, I am very sorry for it, and I wish to know on what terms I may be restored to your favour. Shall I ask one of your servants ? He knows nothing at all about the matter. He can give nothing better than conjecture. You, my dear sir, the person injured, you only can tell me on what terms I may be restored to your favour. Even so, in the very nature of the case, it is none but God himself who can satisfactorily answer the question, How can a man be just with God ? And yet the infidel laughs at the idea of a Divine revelation, and plumes himself upon being a reasonable man ! Not so very reasonable after all ! Mark my word —not so very reasonable after all ! But,

2. If the Bible be not Divinely inspired, herein is another marvellous thing to be accounted for—

that somehow or other this blessed volume
answers all the purposes of a Divine revelation.
to say nothing of its giving an account, and the
only rational account, of the creation of the world,
of the origin of sin, of the division of time into
weeks of seven days, of the deluge, and other
matters connected with the early history of the
globe; is it not remarkable that the Bible answers
most clearly and satisfactorily the questions propounded, as we have stated, by human nature
itself?

Take the first question, Where is God, my
Maker? or, What is God? You recollect the
reply of Simonides to the monarch who propounded to him the question: " Sire, the more I
think upon this subject, the more I am lost in its
difficulty and immensity." Now ask the disciple
whom Jesus loved the same question, What is
God? "God is love," says he. How beautiful!
how sublime! But if you wish a more extended
view of the Divine character, according to the
Scriptures, "God is a Spirit, infinite, eternal, and
unchangeable, in his being, wisdom, power, holi-
ness, justice, goodness, and truth." Can any
description of the Supreme Being be nobler and
more perfect than this? And, being drawn from
the Bible, is not this "a stamp divine"? Are
not these "credentials clear"? And yet the
infidel rejects the sacred volume—and, doubtless,

he is a very reasonable man! In intellect, a son
of Anak—head and shoulders taller than all
around him! "Oh, shame! where is thy
blush?"

But another question, as we have said, which
human nature asks with well-grounded solicitude,
is this—How can a man be just with God? How
can a man, who is a sinner, obtain the forgiveness
of his sins, and be restored to the favour of his
Maker? Sages of ancient times, and wise ones
of the present day, will talk, as we have said,
about the merit of penances and pilgrimages, and
lay great stress upon the efficacy of repentance and
reformation; but these things have no Divine
warrant; they are, at best, only matters of conjecture, and all the evidence of analogy is against
them.

Here is a man who, by a course of licentious
indulgence and extravagance, has lost his healtl
and property; and I find that neither penances,
nor pilgrimages, nor repentance, nor reformation,
nor all of them united, will remove the effects of
his licentiousness and extravagance. How do I
know, then, that they can remove the penal consequences of sin?

In the very nature of the case, none but God
can tell on what terms He will pardon the sinner,
and receive him to favour; for none but He can
tell what the honour of the Divine government

may require, or how the punishment of the offender can be remitted, without endangering the tranquillity of other worlds and creatures which He has made.

Now, on the subject of forgiveness and restoration to the favour of God, the Bible is remarkably clear, and full, and express. Thus Paul, addressing the men of Antioch, says, " Be it known unto you, therefore, men and brethren, that through this Man, Christ Jesus, is preached unto you the forgiveness of sins ; and by Him all that believe are justified from all things, from which ye could not be justified by the law of Moses." Again, writing to Timothy, he says, " It is a faithful saying, and worthy of all acceptation, that Christ Jesus came into the world to save sinners, of whom I am chief." And again, writing to the Romans, we find him using this language, " Therefore, being justified by faith, we have peace with God, through our Lord Jesus Christ ; by whom also we have received the atonement." And again, " There is therefore now no condemnation to them which are in Christ Jesus, who walk not after the flesh, but after the Spirit." And all this beautifully harmonizes with the words of the Lord Jesus Christ himself, " God so loved the world, that He gave his only-begotten Son, that whosoever believeth in Him should not perish, but have everlasting life."

How delightful are these declarations! What light do they give to the inquiring sinner—what sweet relief to the burdened soul!

3. If the Bible be not Divinely inspired, here is another marvellous thing—that it furnishes a perfect code of moral precepts. In this it is perfectly unique, and stands alone in its glory; for I am bold to say, that there is no other volume upon the face of the earth which furnishes such a code of precepts. Those acquainted with the writings of heathen sages and moralists know full well, that their ideas on the subject of moral obligation are remarkably crude, some sanctioning suicide and some infanticide; and even the enlightened and comparatively virtuous Cicero says, "It is lawful to fight for glory." And what is this but sanctioning ambition? Ambition! the direct tendency of which is to drench the earth in blood, and fill the world with widows and orphans! The Bible, thank God, teaches a purer and better morality than this!

We said that it furnishes a perfect code of moral precepts. We do not declaim, we give proof, absolute demonstration. Our Saviour sums up all the precepts of the sacred volume in two great commandments. *First,* Thou shalt love the Lord thy God with all thy heart, and soul, and mind, and strength; and, *secondly,* Thou shalt love thy neighbour as thyself. Now, these two command-

ments embrace every duty that can be required
of man.

Take the *first*. We are to love the Lord our
God supremely; see how this embraces every duty
which we owe to our Maker. For example, am I
required to submit to God? How easy and how
natural it is to submit to one whom we supremely
love! Am I required to repent of my sins? It
is love which breaks the heart, which melts it down
in tender relentings for sin! Am I required to
choose God as the portion of my soul? If I love
Him supremely, I have done it already. Am I
required to obey all his commandments? And
who does not know that

> " 'Tis loves which makes our cheerful feet
>   In swift obedience move?"

Take the *second* great commandment, Thou
shalt love thy neighbour as thyself. Only let this
precept be acted upon in all the length and breadth
of its requirement, and, verily, there would be no
occasion for bolts, nor bars, nor jails, nor penitentiaries, nor anything of the kind. "Love,"
says the apostle, " worketh no ill to his neighbour, therefore love is the fulfilling of the law."
Yes, only let the great law of love be acted upon,
in all the length and breadth of its requirements,
and man would become an angel and earth a
paradise!

To crown the whole, strange as it may seem,

all duties both toward God and man are, in the Bible, embraced in a single word; and that, how simple, how well understood by the learned and the unlearned; by the civilized, by the barbarian; by male and female; by the child of three years of age and the man of threescore and ten—Love! For *love*, says the apostle, is the fulfilling of the law. Is not this a stamp Divine? Are not these credentials clear? Yet the infidel rejects the Bible! Let him write a better book if he can!

And this reminds me of the case of Lord Lyttelton, who, belonging to a club of infidels, was selected to burn the Bible. Taking the volume in his hand, he approached the hearth, but, upon second thought, returned and replaced the book upon the stand. When asked why he did not throw it into the fire, he made this very sensible remark, "We will not burn this book until we can get a better." Verily, "their rock is not as our Rock, even our enemies themselves being judges." Again—

4. If the Bible be not Divinely inspired, is it not very strange and unaccountable that so many miracles were wrought in illustration of its truths? Miracles wrought in open day; in the presence of enemies; and subjected to the severest scrutiny. Now, either these miracles were wrought, or they were not: if wrought, the case is settled: for they are the clearest credentials of the Divine mis-

sion of those who wrought them. If not wrought, how comes it to pass, that we have such a particular and detailed account of them ? How comes it to pass, that they were attested by so many eyewitnesses, many of whom suffered martyrdom in attestation of the facts which they affirmed ? Moreover, how comes it to pass that these miracles had so powerful an influence in the spreading of doctrines so directly opposed to long-established systems and the passions of men ? And, let it not be forgotten, that, in commemoration of some of these miracles, we have monuments and memorials brought down even to the present time : the Sabbath, for example, changed from the seventh to the first day of the week. This is a standing monument of that stupendous miracle, the resurrection of Christ, which it commemorates. And yet the infidel wants proof ! Once more—

5. If the blessed volume before me be not Divinely inspired, how shall we account for the fact that it contains some five or six hundred prophecies which have been most literally and remarkably fulfilled ? All this occurs in the sermon on Fulfilment of Prophecy (p. 34). For example: of Ishmael it was predicted, that he should become a great nation ; that he should be a wild man, and that his hand should be against every man, and every man's hand against him ; and that he should

dwell in the presence of all his brethren (Gen.
xvi. 12); that is, should never be subdued, or
brought into subjection. Those acquainted with
the Arabs know that these predictions have been
fulfilled to the very letter; and with regard to the
independence which they should ever maintain, it
is remarkable, that, although special efforts have
been made by powerful monarchs in various ages
to put them down, these efforts have all, ulti-
mately, proved unsuccessful. Sesostris, Cyrus,
Pompey, Trajan, and many other great conque-
rors, aimed at subjugating them, but never succeeded. At the present day, the Arabs, although
wandering and predatory, are still an independent
people; like the wild ass, whose home is the wilderness, whose pasture is the mountains, and who
searcheth after every green thing.

The prophecies in relation to Nineveh, Baby-
lon, Tyre, and Egypt, have also received the most
exact accomplishment; their present condition,
according to the statements of modern travellers,
being precisely what was predicted so many thousand years ago. With regard to Egypt, I will
mention a fact which may have escaped the notice
of some: Egypt, says the prophet Ezekiel (xxix.
15) shall not exalt itself any more above the
nations. This was a bold prophecy, when we
consider when it was uttered; but the subsequent
history of Egypt has been in exact accordance

with the prediction. But the particular point to which I refer is this : Not a great many years since, Mehemet Ali, the Pacha of Egypt, was upon the very point of subverting the Turkish empire; and would have done it, had not the sovereigns of Russia, Prussia, Austria, and Great Britain interposed. And this they did, mark ! not to accomplish the prophecy, but to preserve the balance of power.

The prophecies which relate to the *Messiah* are about two hundred in number, which have in every particular been exactly fulfilled, in our blessed Redeemer. Let me mention only a very few.* It was predicted of Him that He should be despised and rejected by his own people, the Jews ; that He should lift up a standard to the Gentiles ; to Him should the gathering of the Gentiles be: and in Him shall the Gentiles trust.

Now this is prophecy. What is history? In exact accordance with the prophecy. Was Christ to be despised and rejected by his own people; the Jews ? He came unto his own, says John, and his own received Him not. And they, that is, the Jews, says Luke, were instant with loud voices in the temple, requiring that He might be crucified. Was Christ to lift up a standard to the Gentiles ? And was not Saul of Tarsus converted, and made

* Isa. liii. 3; xlix. 22; Gen. xlix. 10 ; xi. 10; Matt. xii. 17—21.

the great apostle of the Gentiles? Moreover, to Him was the gathering of the Gentiles to be. And who are they now who profess the Christian faith? Are they not Gentiles? Few Jews, but many Gentiles. On the morning of the Christian Sabbath, the doors of ten thousand sanctuaries are thrown open, and see the multitudes who gather around the standard of the cross! Are they Jews?—are they not Gentiles? But it is added: In Him shall the Gentiles trust. We are all Gentiles, I suppose, who are here to-day; and now tell me, my brother, my sister—O ye precious sons and daughters of Zion! tell me, in whom do you trust for salvation? Is it not in the crucified Nazarene? And in whom did that dear mother of yours trust in a dying hour, when she so sweetly smiled, and said to you, "Meet me in heaven"—in whom did she trust? Was it not in Him who by the Jews was despised and rejected? I too am a Gentile, and I am not ashamed to say, that this same blessed Saviour is my only hope. Give me Christ, or else I die.

This day, then, have we evidence before our own eyes, and in our own hearts, that the prophecies are true and the Bible is true. Yet the infidel rejects the sacred volume! And why? Oh, because he is a reasonable man, and he cannot, without a prostration of everything like reason, embrace a system so preposterous and absurd!

Ah! if I mistake not, when afflictions shall make him more sober, and the near prospect of death shall make him more thoughtful, he will then see the evidence of the truth of the Bible more clearly than he does now! Like Ethan Allen, who, being asked by a dying daughter whether she should believe what her pious mother had taught her or he? replied with tears, " My daughter, you had better believe what your mother has taught you." Oh, how plain it is, and how appropriate is our text: " Their rock is not as our Rock, even our enemies themselves being judges."

II. The supreme excellence or decided superiority of the Christian religion appears also in reference to its moral influence. And here, if I mistake not, we have public sentiment fully on our side: let a thorough-going infidel be truly converted and become a real Christian; will not all persons expect to see an improvement in his moral character? But, on the other hand, let a real Christian (if it were possible) become a thorough-going infidel, and is there a man upon the face of the earth who anticipates an improvement in his moral character? Would there not rather be a suspicion waked up in the bosoms of all, that that man had become loose in his morals, and, therefore, had become loose in his sentiments?

Even the infidel himself is frequently constrained to pay homage to the Christian system, in relation to its moral influence. For example—here is an infidel about to die; he makes his will, and, greatly desiring that his children should not be defrauded, he wishes to fix upon some honest man to act as executor; would he not rather select a man that he believes to be a real and consistent Christian, than an open and avowed infidel ?   Now these things speak volumes. The fact is, the general sentiment is this, that however imperfect some professors of religion may be, yet Christianity itself is most excellent: that it elevates the standard of morals, and has a direct and powerful tendency to purify the heart and improve the character of all who are really and truly brought under its moral influence; and hence it is expected to make better husbands and better wives, better parents and better children, better masters and better servants ; yea, better altogether.

This is the general sentiment; and I will now show that this general sentiment is well based. This we would argue from the character of its precepts, and the power of its motives.

First, from the character of its precepts. It is evident, the more perfect the precepts the more happy their influence upon moral character. We have shown that the precepts of the Bible bear the stamp of absolute perfection ; of course, then, so far as good precepts can influence the character of man, the influence of the precepts of the sacred volume must be most happy. But to place this in, perhaps, a stronger point of light, observe, there are three principles of action—fear, interest, and love. Fear, as a principle of action, is certainly very powerful : but it operates only whilst the rod is extended. Interest is also a very powerful principle, but this principle is not strong enough to meet many cases ; for a man may know what is right, yet do what is wrong ; he may know that a certain course of conduct will promote his highest interests, but the principle of interest fail to rule him, not being strong enough. But there is one principle yet remaining, *love ;* and that we may understand its true nature and power, see that tender mother—she has a beloved Joseph, or some dear little Benjamin, who is very, very sick. See the mother of that child ! I can tell you where you can find her, by night and by day ;—not in the store, nor in her neighbour's house, nor even in the sanctuary ; no ! but by the couch of her suffering child !

Now what is it that binds her to that place ? What is it that makes her so kind and unremitting in her attentions ? Is it fear ? There is no rod over her. Is it interest ? The idea of interest never once enters her mind. What is it then ? Why it is love ? Yes, it is love which binds her to the couch of her suffering child. It is love which makes her take a positive pleasure in performing the most menial offices for the poor little sufferer. Take away that mother (it will require a strong arm to do this!)—reach out the arm of a Hercules, and tear away that mother—substitute a hireling. Bring rewards and punishments to bear upon that hireling to their greatest possible extent, and I will venture to affirm, that there is no hireling on earth that will take a mother's place. And why? For this simple reason—the mother is under the influence of the strongest feeling which can animate the human bosom— love.

Verily there is no principle of action like it, so strong, so uniform, so lasting! and, moreover, who does not know that the service which love prompts is of all others the most pleasant and desirable? Now is it not remarkable that, in our religion, this is made the great principle of moral action. Yes, not fear, nor interest, but love. Love, says the apostle, is the fulfilling of the law. And to make the matter yet more remarkable, this principle being fixed upon, to wake it up and give it new power and energy over the human soul, God himself has set us an example of love in giving us his Son, his only-begotten and well-beloved Son, to die for our redemption.

And now, candid man, speak! Does not this look like a religion which comes from God? If any religion can have a happy influence upon moral character, must it not be that religion, all the precepts of which are summed up in *love?* Yet the infidel wants proof!

. With regard to the motives which are, in the Bible, brought to bear upon the moral character of man, they are absolutely the strongest which can exist. This is no rhetorical figure, no idle declamation; it is simple, undeniable fact. Here is the demonstration. Are the motives to virtuous living drawn in the Scriptures, from God ? They are; and now, is there any god in the universe greater than the God whom the Bible reveals ? Are they drawn from the joys of heaven ? They are; and are there any joys greater than the joys of heaven ? Are they drawn from the torments of the damned in hell ? They are; and are there any torments more tormenting than the torments of the damned in hell ? Are they drawn from the love of Christ ? They are ; and is there any love so strong, so touching, so soul-subduing, as the love of Christ, who, according to the Scriptures, died on the cross for us? Are the motives drawn from eternity ? They are; and is there any duration longer than that of eternity ?

Thus you perceive that the motives to holy living, in the Bible, are not only drawn from three worlds, heaven, earth, and hell, in short from all quarters, but they are literally and absolutely the strongest which, in the very nature of the case, can be brought to bear upon the moral character of man. The fact is, Christianity goes in advance, lays the hand of a master upon every source of motive, and monopolizes them all.

And now, suppose that Infidelity would urge motives to holy living (which, however, is not very probable), whence will it derive its motives? from God? The infidel is not very certain that there is a God. Will infidelity draw its motives from the joys of heaven? These, he suspects, are only the dreams of the visionary enthusiast. Shall motives be drawn from the torments of hell? The infidel is quite sure that there is no such place as that. Shall motives be drawn from love? Alas! infidelity presents, in its system, no dying Saviour, no cross crimsoned with atoning blood! Shall the motives then be drawn from eternity? The infidel strongly suspects that death is an eternal sleep.

Oh, what a poor thing infidelity is, when seen in the undress of its true character! How lean! how haggard! how shrivelled! ay, and may I not add, how frightful, too! I have mentioned, that if Christianity should universally prevail, if its precepts were acted upon in all the length and breadth of their requirements, there would be no occasion for bolts, nor bars, nor jails, nor penitentiaries, nor anything of the kind, for man would become as an angel, and earth a paradise. But if, on the other hand, infidelity should prevail does any man in his senses believe that there would be no occasion for bolts, nor bars, nor jails, nor penitentiaries, nor anything of the kind?—that man would become as an angel, or earth a paradise? I think not.

In the providence of God infidelity did once prevail—*where?* In revolutionary France—*when?* During that period, so properly called, " the reign of terror." Yes, infidelity did then prevail, for at that time the National Convention decreed that there was no God. The Sabbath was abolished : churches were turned into temples of reason: death was declared to be an eternal sleep; and the Bible was dragged along the streets of Lyons in derision and contempt.

Yes, I repeat it, infidelity then prevailed, and verily its fruits were the fruits of Sodom, and its clusters the clusters of Gomorrah. Infidelity then reigned, and most frightful was its reign. Its crown was terror; its throne, the guillotine; its sceptre, the battle-axe; its palace-yard, a field of blood; and its royal robes dripped, and dripped, and dripped, with human gore. All France was,' as it were, one vast slaughter-house, and the rulers of France, as demons from the bottomless pit. " O my soul, come not thou into their secret; unto their assembly, mine honour, be not thou united." "Their rock is not as our Rock, even our enemies themselves being judges." But,

III. The supreme excellence and decided superiority of the Christian religion appears in reference to the happiness of man. What has a favourable influence upon human character, must also have a favourable influence upon human happiness, for these things are linked together like the balloon and its car : the ascent of the one, necessarily leads to the elevation of the other.

That the Christian religion is favourable to human happiness, is, I believe, the secret conviction, even of many who may not openly confess it; hence it is no uncommon thing to hear even the openly wicked say, " I believe that the real Christian is the happiest man in the world : " and I recollect the remark of a certain sceptic, made to myself (it was in the hour of affliction), " Oh, sir, you Christians have the advantage of ' *us !* ' "

I think I may venture then to affirm, that general sentiment is on our side ; and I think I can show that this general sentiment is well based, for what does the Christian religion do ? It subdues the boisterous passions of the soul ; converts the lion into a lamb ; the vulture into a dove : must not this be favourable to human happiness ?

What does the Christian religion do ? It gives exercise to gracious affections. Instead of encouraging anger, wrath, malice, revenge, and other hateful and soul-tormenting passions, it disposes its subject to be kind, gentle, affectionate, and forgiving; and must not this be favourable to human happiness?

What does the Christian religion do? It sheds abroad a Saviour's love in the heart; gives the sweet assurance that our sins are all forgiven for Jesus' sake; that the eternal God is our Father; that heaven is our home; and that, if the earthly house of this our tabernacle be dissolved, we have a building of God, a house not made with hands, eternal and on high.

Oh, it is a blessed thing to be a Christian; even "if it be a delusion," as one remarks, "it is a sweet delusion," and, "if false, no truth so precious as the lie." Oh, see the young convert, whose evidences are bright and clear, how happy! and see the dying Christian, who leaves the world in the full hope of glory, how triumphant! The Pentecostal converts, we are told, did eat their meat with gladness and singleness of heart, praising God; and when many believed in Samaria, we also learn that there was great joy in that city. And the beauty of the thing is this, that when afflictions come and comforts are most needed, then the consolations of religion are strongest and most abundant, for religion teaches every child of God that afflictions are all ordered in mercy, and are but the sterner voice of God's parental love. Yes! and in the darkest hour,

" Here speaks the Comforter, in God's name, saying,
Earth has no sorrows that Heaven cannot cure."

This, my brethren, is certainly a great thing for man in this vale of tears—in this land of trials, troubles, disappointments, sickness, sorrow, and death. Ah! how many sad scenes of mourning are presented in this sorrowful world of ours! Here some venerated father cries out, with the patriarch of old, " My Joseph is no more! and my grey hairs must go down with sorrow to the grave!" There some tender mother weeps over the darling of her bosom, as she commits its clay-cold form to its narrow house. Here some affectionate husband laments the untimely death of the wife of his bosom, the jewel of his heart; and there some devoted wife mingles bitter tears with the clods which rest upon the bosom of the dear one she loved—her husband. How distressing!

But perhaps this is not all; she is made the widowed mother of poor fatherless children, who look up to her for comfort and support, and look in vain. The prop, the only support of the family, is taken away! and they, what shall they do? The heart, bursting with grief, vents its complaints, it murmurs and repines, " Where is the compassion of my God? where are the tender mercies of my heavenly Father? my affliction is too much for my wounded spirit! it is more than I can bear! would God I had never been born!

or would God I were with my beloved, sleeping
with him in his silent grave!" Cease, mourner!
cease thy complaints! says our religion. It is
God, why weepest thou? Remember, He is a
God of unerring wisdom and boundless compassion. Know this—enough for thee to know—God
does not willingly afflict the children of men, but
chastens and rebukes in covenant love. Cease,
mourner! cease thy complaints! thy heavenly
Father speaks to thee, " Silence, my child! what
I do thou knowest not now, but thou shalt know
hereafter." Oh, how does this soothe the smitten
heart, and wipe away the falling tears! Verily,
the consolations of religion are sweet and strong,
fulfilling the words of the Psalmist, " God is our
refuge and strength, a very present help in time of
trouble."

"How do you find yourself this morning?"
said a certain pastor to a beloved female member
of his church who was near her end. Grasping
the hand of her pastor, she replied, "I am in
great pain, but, oh, I am happy—very happy!"

How different was it with Hume's mother,
who, when in deep affliction, said to her son,
" My son, you have taken away my religion, and
now tell me something to comfort me;" but no
comfort could he give, and none could she receive.
" God of Queen Clotilda," cried out the infidel
Clovis I. of France, when in trouble on the field

of battle, "God of Queen Clotilda! grant me the victory!" Why did he not call upon his own God? Saunderson, who was a great admirer of Sir Isaac Newton's talents, and who made light of his religion in health, was, nevertheless, heard to say in dismal accents on a dying bed, "God of Sir Isaac Newton, have mercy on me!" Why this changing of gods in a dying hour?

And it is a remarkable fact, if an infidel have a wife who is a Christian, he is very willing, in case of her death, to have the minister attending her funeral to say, " My friends, here we have a daughter of Zion shrouded and prepared for the burying. You all knew her very well. She was a Christian; she lived the life of the Christian; she died the Christian's death, and is gone to the Christian's rest, the pilgrim's home."

But, suppose this wife of his had been as thorough-going an infidel as himself, and the minister at her funeral should say, "My friends, here is one before us shrouded and prepared for the burying. You all knew her well. She was a thorough-going infidel. She lived the life of an infidel, died his death, and is gone to his place!" Would this please him? Nay, verily, for there are certain seasons when the mind will be sober, and the voice of truth will be heard! You have heard, no doubt, of many an infidel on a dying bed wishing that he was a good Christian; but did you ever hear of a single Christian on a dying bed wishing that he was a good infidel? No! never! never! never! The case is clear. "Their rock is not as our Rock, even our enemies themselves being judges."

Well, my brethren, we must all die. We all wish to die happy—certainly, at least, on the safe side. Now let it be remembered, that whilst the bed of death is most generally a terrible place for the infidel, "the chamber where the Christian meets his fate, is privileged beyond the common walks of virtuous life, quite on the verge of heaven."

Here, we will suppose, is a dormitory on the right, where Christians are breathing their last. Here, on the left, is another dormitory, in which infidels are giving up the ghost. Let us visit, first, the dormitory upon the right. Who is that who is just expiring? It is the pious Halyburton. How serene, how calm! But he is going to speak. Hark! let us catch some of his last words. "It is no easy thing to be a Christian," says he, "but, by the grace of God, I have got the victory! Now I know, I feel, I believe, I rejoice. I feed on manna! I have angels' food! Mine eyes shall see my Redeemer. Oh, the glory, the unspeakable glory! My heart is full, my heart is full!"

" Sure the last end
Of the good man is peace !   How calm his exit !
Night dews fall not more gently to the ground ;
Nor weary, worn out winds expire so soft !"

" Let me die the death of the righteous, and let my last end be like his."

Now, let us pass over to the dormitory on the left.   Who is that just expiring ?   It is the wretched Altamont (a fictitious name, but descriptive of a real case).   Oh, how distorted are his features, and how full of agony does he seem to be.   The clock strikes, and he exclaims, " Oh, time, time ! it is fit that thou shouldst thus strike thy murderer to the heart !   How art thou fled for ever !   A month ! a day ! I ask not for years, though an age were too little to fit me for the work which I have to do."   Another groan, and he cries out in anguish unutterable : " My principles have poisoned my friend ! my extravagance has beggared my boy ! my unkindness has murdered my wife !   And is there another hell ?   O thou blasphemed, yet indulgent Lord God ! hell itself is a refuge if it hide me from thy frown !"   Here we have, even on earth, the first notes of the wailings of the lost in the world to come !

Tell me not of the peaceful death of David Hume.   His nurse has told some tales of horror —but let that pass.   How did he die, as the most favourable account represents ?   He died playing

at cards, and jesting about Charon and his boat.
Does it become the dignity of man, òr the solem-
nity of the hour of dissolution, in any case, .to
leave the world in this way ?   Believe me, it was
only a desperate effort to bar serious thought !—
like the schoolboy, passing through the graveyard
at night, with satchel in his hand,

> "Whistling aloud to bear his courage up."

Thank God, the Christian has no occasion for
any artficial excitement of this kind, for, to him,
"to die is gain."   Do you demand further proof?
Let us make another visit to the dormitory on the
right.   How pleasant is everything around this
hallowed spot?   Who is that just sinking in the
arms of death?   It is Edward Payson.   Oh, how
happy he looks.   But he is going to speak ; what
is his language ?   " I am going to Mount Zion,"
says he, " I am going 'to the city of the living
God, the heavenly Jerusalem ! to an innumerable
company of angels, to the general assembly and
church of the first-born, whose names are written
in heaven.'   I swim in a river of pleasure ! I swim
in a flood of glory !"

    And who is that in the next chamber, who is
bidding his friends a final adieu?   It is William
C. Walton, the associate of my college days ; and
what are his dying words ?   They are very beautiful and very sweet.   " The sting of death is
gone," says he, " the grave is disrobed of its ter-

rors! Peace like a river flows into my soul! I am now in the Jordan of death, and blessed be God, its waters do not cover me. I shall see Jesus! See JESUS! what a thought that is! Oh, glorious Saviour!"

Surely, my brethren, the curtains of light and glory are hung around this dormitory; but around the dormitory on the left, the curtains of gloom and despair. Over this waves the white banner of the Prince of Peace. Over that the black banner of Apollyon! Here are choirs of angels waiting to sing the pilgrim to his rest. There ministers of vengeance, ready to hurry the guilty soul of the dying sinner, reluctantly, oh how reluctantly! before thy throne, thrice holy God.

And now, my dear friends, one and all remember, we must die: we cannot help it; and remember, after death comes the judgment, and once lost, lost for ever. When Death's leaden sceptre is laid upon our cold bosoms, no mistakes can be rectified any more; for, so soon as the breath leaves the body, the decree of an immutable God rolls over the shrouded form. "He that is filthy, let him be filthy still; and he that is holy, let him be holy still." In which dormitory would you rather die? Immortal man, take care! great interests are at stake—see to it, that you be upon the safe side; for, I repeat it, *once lost, you are lost for ever.*

THE FULFILMENT OF SCRIPTURE PROPHECY.

"For the prophecy came not in old time by the will of man; but holy men of God spake as they were moved by the Holy Ghost."—2 PET. i. 21.

WHEN the apostle Peter wrote this, his second and last epistle, being aware that he must soon go the way of all the earth, he seems to have been particularly desirous that his Christian brethren should distinctly bear in mind one thing—that they had "not followed cunningly devised fables;" that the Saviour whom they received was indeed the predicted Messiah, and consequently the religion which he promulgated was true—was divinely true. With regard to himself, if there were no other evidence of the fact, the transfiguration scene was of itself sufficiently convincing, for he was an eye-witness of his majesty, when there came such a voice from the excellent glory, saying, "This is my beloved Son, in whom I am well pleased."

"But," continues he, "we have a more sure word of prophecy, whereunto ye do well to take heed, as to a light shining in a dark place, until the day dawn, and the day-star arise in your hearts." The main idea here seems to be this: while the miraculous attestation given to the character of Christ on the mount of transfiguration was abundantly sufficient to satisfy himself and others who were eye-witnesses on the occasion, it might not be convincing to such as had not been present, and therefore he refers them to what he denominates the more sure word of prophecy— more sure, because more capable of being more deliberately and severely tested. You perceive, my brethren, that the apostle lays great stress upon prophecy, as furnishing a powerful argument for the truth of the Christian religion; and I am free to say that I do think it furnishes an argument which can neither be gainsayed nor resisted; an argument which can bear the most thorough examination, and which will stand the "test of scrutiny, of talents, and of time."

I. In relation to Abraham, when he was aged, and yet childless, and Sarah his wife, also well stricken in age, it was predicted that his seed should be exceedingly numerous. "If," said God, "a man can number the dust of the earth, then shall thy seed also be numbered." About four hundred years after this, the children of Israel (only a portion of his posterity) came out of Egypt, and encamped in the plains of Moab, an exceeding great multitude. Balak, king of Moab, alarmed for the safety of his dominions, sends for Balaam, the prophet of Aram — and mark what is said : " Behold there is a people come out of Egypt : behold they cover the face of the earth ! Come now, I pray thee, and curse me this people, for they are too mighty for me." When Balaam came, having erected his altars and offered sacrifices, he took up his parable and said—mark his language !—" Balak, king of Moab, hath brought me from Aram, out of the mountains of the East, saying, Come, curse me Jacob, and come, defy Israel. How shall I curse whom God hath not cursed ? and how shall I defy, whom the Lord hath not defied ? From the top of the rocks I see him, and from the hills I behold him ! Lo, this people shall dwell alone, and not be reckoned among the nations ! Who can count the dust of Jacob, or the number of the fourth part of Israel ?" Here you perceive that the thing which particularly struck the prophet of Aram was the exceeding great number of the people spread out before him.

But there is another prophecy in relation to Abraham, which is perhaps still more remarkable. It is this : *I will make thy name great in the earth.* Now, let it be remembered, that when this language was uttered, Abraham was but a plain man, dwelling in tents. He was no statesman, no warrior; he was no poet, no orator. There was nothing about him which promised to twine around his brow the laurels of fame; nothing whatever which seemed calculated to stamp his character with immortality. He was only, as we have said, a plain man, dwelling in tents; and yet it was predicted that his name should be great in the earth.

And has not this prophecy been literally fulfilled? Is not his name great in the earth at the present time? Has it not been great for, lo! these many thousand years? Most of the nations of the East endeavour to trace up their genealogy to this wonderful man. With regard to the Jews, his lineal descendants, we all know how proud they are of him as their great progenitor; and even we Gentile Christians, made the children of Abraham by faith, even we also have for him a most profound veneration.

Tell me, my brethren, who and where is the man, and in what age did he ever live, whose name is to be compared with that of Abraham? We have heard of Nebuchadnezzar the Great, and Pompey the Great, and Alexander the Great, and Herod, and Frederick, and Napoleon the Great; but the name of Abraham is far greater than each—far greater than all! Is not this remarkable? Is it not strong proof of the inspiration of the sacred volume? Young man, your mother is right! The Bible is true. Beware how you slight it! It will cost you your soul!

II. In Genesis ix. 27, we have a very remarkable prophecy, uttered by Noah: "God shall enlarge Japheth: he shall dwell in the tents of Shem; and Canaan shall be his servant." The first thing, in relation to this prophecy, which we would notice, is this, that here, in three sentences, embracing only twenty words, Noah sketches the outline of the history of the whole human race, descending from his three sons, Shem, Ham and Japheth.

Notice each prediction: "God shall enlarge Japheth." Dr. Scott says that Japheth seems to have been the progenitor of more than one-half of the human family! Besides occupying a large part of Asia, they spread all over Europe. They swarm in the West India Islands, and nearly cover all America, north and south. Thus, in exact accordance with the prophecy, God *has* enlarged Japheth.

But it is also said, "He shall dwell in the tents of Shem." Now, whether this prophecy has relation to political or religious privileges, it has been most remarkably fulfilled. It is well known, that political power has, to a great extent, passed over from the children of Shem to the children of Japheth; and in religious matters also (the gospel, for example), we see with our own eyes that Japheth has supplanted Shem. The Jews, for their unbelief, have been cut off, and we Gentiles, and children of Japheth, have been brought in. The aborigines of this country, beyond all doubt, are the children of Shem; and have not the children of Japheth, passing over from the Old World, here on this Western Continent, literally taken possession of the tents of Shem? Where your house now stands was once an Indian wigwam; and where our cities now rise in splendour, were seen, two centuries ago, the villages of the red men of the West. Yes, by treaty and by conquest, by fair means and foul means, the children of Japheth have lorded it over the children of Shem, and are at this very time dwelling in their tents.

But the prophet adds, "And Canaan shall be his servant." And where, I would ask, do those in servitude chiefly come from, if not from Africa, the home of Ham, the father of Canaan? Ham, it seems, has never shaken a sceptre over Japheth. Shem has subdued Japheth, and Japheth has subdued Shem; but Ham has subdued neither. And thus we see that each item of Noah's prophecy has been most remarkably fulfilled. "God shall enlarge Japheth; he shall dwell in the tents of Shem; and Canaan shall be his servant." How is this to be accounted for?

Peter tells, " Prophecy came not in old time by the will of man ; but holy men of God spake as they were moved by the Holy Ghost."

III. The next remarkable prophecy to which I shall call your attention, is found in Exodus xxxiv. 24 : "Neither shall any man desire thy land when thou shalt go up to appear before the Lord thy God, thrice in the year."

By reference to the context, it will be seen that Moses had given directions, that when the children of Israel had taken possession of the promised land, there should be a gathering together of the men, 'from all their coasts, to worship at one altar thrice in every year. Anticipating an objection which might very naturally be made, that this would hold out a temptation to lawless and predatory bands to take advantage of the occasion to rob and plunder, Moses, to set them at rest upon this point, utters the bold prophecy recited : "Neither shall any man desire thy land, when thou shalt go up to appear before the Lord thy God, thrice in the year."

Now, this prophecy was either fulfilled, or not fulfilled. If not, how shall we account for the fact —the well known fact—that year after year, and age after age, the males did go up to Jerusalem with their offerings, as directed. Suppose, for example, relying upon the protecting providence of God, promised by Moses, they had gone up, and upon

their return, had found that this protecting providence had not been vouchsafed, think you that
they would have gone up again? I suspect not.
They would have seen that an imposition of a
very serious character had been practised upon
them; and one imposition of this kind would
have sufficed. They would have gone up and
left their families and possessions defenceless no
more.

Now, the question is, how could Moses, how
could any uninspired man, have foreseen that such
a remarkable (may I not say miraculous) providence would be spreading its protecting shield over
them year after year? This is truly a very remarkable case, and is worthy of the serious thought
of every sceptic in the land. It furnishes an
argument for the truth of the Bible, which I
humbly conceive cannot be set aside. Yes, the
Bible is true! Thank God, it comes to us with
" credentials clear," " on every line marked with
the seal of high divinity."

IV. In the ninth chapter of the book of Daniel,
from the 24th verse to the close of that chapter,
we have a rich cluster of prophecies in relation to
the Messiah. We will point out only two or
three, and those the fulfilment of which is remarkably clear and manifest. 1. It was predicted that
He, the true Messiah, when He came, should cause
the sacrifice and oblation to cease. Was not this

a very strange prediction ?   Shall cause the sacrifice and oblation to cease!   Were not these of
Divine appointment ?   Did they not form the very
sum and substance of the Jew's religion ?   How
unlikely was the fulfilment of this prediction !
And yet, has it not been literally fulfilled ?   Christ,
by his death upon the cross, superseded the necessity of all the Levitical sacrifices under the law.
"It is finished," said He, as He bowed his head
upon the cross, and the old dispensation then
passed away.   No acceptable sacrifice was offered
after that : ay, and soon the very altar was de-
molished — and lo ! the sacrificial fire has been
quenched for these eighteen hundred years !   It is
well known that sacrifices and offerings were permitted to be made in Jerusalem only.   This holy
city, having passed over into the hands of the Gentiles, the sacrifice and offering have literally ceased,
even down to the present day, so that we can see
the fulfilment of this prophecy with our own eyes.

One of these predictions is this : " He shall
seal up the vision and the prophecy."   That is,
shall close the sacred canon.   Turn to the last
chapter of the book of Revelation, and you will
find these words : " If any man shall add unto
these things, God shall add unto him the plagues
that are written in this book."   And mark who
the speaker is : " I, Jesus, have sent mine angel
to testify unto you these things in the churches."

Here you perceive the blessed Saviour, the true Messiah (just as it was predicted so long time ago), with authority, closes the sacred canon.

It is true—the papal Council of Trent, in the sixteenth century, had the hardihood and daring wickedness to add the Apocrypha (books which the Jews themselves never received as inspired), and what was this? Evidence that the prophecy was not fulfilled by Christ, as the Messiah? Nay, verily, but proof positive that the papal church, thus trampling upon the authority of Christ, is, in deed and in truth, the antichristian power, which itself also was predicted.

A third prediction in this connection is this: " The people of the prince that shall come shall destroy the city and the sanctuary." And who is this prince, in whose day the city and the sanctuary were destroyed? Titus, the Roman commander. Was it done by his authority? No, he endeavoured to prevent it. He gave orders to his soldiers to spare the temple; but they were too strong for him. " When they had gotten within the walls of the city," Josephus states, " they were seized with a kind of frenzy, and, hurling firebrands upon that magnificent edifice, it was, with the city, soon laid in ruins." Note the accuracy of the prediction; not the *prince*, but the *people* of the prince, shall destroy the city and. the sanctuary.

With regard to the seventy weeks spoken of, it is thought to be one of the most remarkable prophecies upon sacred record, and one of those most exactly fulfilled. Almost any commentator will show that the event corresponds to the prediction, to the very letter.

In the forty-fourth chapter of Isaiah, we find another Old Testament prophecy, referring to New Testament times: " I will pour water upon him that is thirsty, and floods upon the dry ground. I will pour my Spirit upon thy seed, and my blessing upon thine offspring : and they shall spring up as among the grass, and as willows by the watercourses." How descriptive is this of those revival scenes which have so signally characterized gospel times, beginning with the outpouring of the Spirit on the day of Pentecost.

The Christian poet, Cowper, thus beautifully describes that still more glorious time :—

" The groans of Nature in this nether world,
   Which heaven has heard for ages, have an end
   Foretold by prophets, and by poets sung,
   Whose fire was kindled at the prophets' lamp,
   The time of rest, the promised sabbath, comes.
   Six thousand years of sorrow have well nigh
   Fulfill'd their tardy and disastrous course
   Over a sinful world ; and what remains
   Of this tempestuous state of human things
   Is merely as the working of a sea
   Before a calm, that rocks itself to rest.
   For He, whose car the winds are, and the clouds

The dust that waits upon his sultry march,
When sin hath moved Him, and his wrath is hot,
Shall visit earth in mercy ; shall descend
Propitious in his chariot paved with love.
O scenes surpassing fable, and yet true,
Scenes of accomplish'd bliss ! which who can see,
Though but in distant prospect, and not feel
His soul refresh'd with foretaste of the joy ?
Rivers of gladness water all the earth,
And clothe all climes with beauty ; the reproach
Of barrenness is past.   The fruitful field
Laughs with abundance ; and the land, once lean,
Or fertile only in its own disgrace,
Exults to see its thistly curse repeal'd ;
The various seasons woven into one,
And that one season an eternal spring.
   Antipathies are none.   No foe to man
Lurks in the serpent now :   the mother sees,
And smiles to see, her infant's playful hand
Stretch'd forth to dally with the crested worm,
To stroke his azure neck, or to receive
The lambent homage of his arrowy tongue.
All creatures worship man, and all mankind
One Lord, one Father.   Error has no place ;
That creeping pestilence is driven away ;
The breath of heaven has chased it.   In the heart
No passion touches a discordant string,
But all is harmony and love.   Disease
Is not : the pure and uncontaminate blood
Holds its due course, nor fears the frost of age.
One song employs all nations ; and all cry,
" Worthy the Lamb, for He was slain for us ! "

V. In the thirty-fifth chapter of Jeremiah we have a prophecy rarely adverted to, and yet one that is exceedingly remarkable. " Jonadab, the son of Rechab, shall not want a man to stand before Me for ever, because he hath obeyed the voice of his father."

The statement of the case is in substance this :—" In the days of Jehoiakim, the son of Josiah, king of Judah, the word of the Lord came unto Jeremiah, saying : Go unto the house of the Rechabites, and bring them into the house of the Lord, into one of the chambers of the priests, and give them wine to drink. And when they were brought in, Jeremiah set before them pots full of wine, and cups, and said unto them, Drink ye wine. But they said, We will drink no wine, for Jonadab the son of Rechab, our father, commanded us, saying, Ye shall drink no wine, neither shall ye build houses, nor sow seed, nor plant vineyards, nor have any, but all your days ye shall dwell in tents ; and we have done according to all that Jonadab our father commanded us. And Jeremiah said unto the house of the Rechabites : Thus saith the Lord of hosts, the God of Israel : Because ye have obeyed the commandment of Jonadab your father, and kept all his precepts, and done according to all that he commanded you, therefore, thus saith the Lord of hosts, the God of Israel, Jonadab, the son of Rechab, shall not want a man to stand before Me for ever ! "

This is the prophecy ; now let us trace its fulfilment.

Some thirty years ago, Joseph Wolf, a missionary to the East, being in Mesopotamia, whilst conversing with the Jews, saw a man standing at a little distance holding a horse by the bridle. "There is one of the Rechabites," said the Jews. Immediately going up to him, the missionary inquired who he was. "I am Mousa," said he; and turning to the thirty-fifth chapter of Jeremiah, in a Bible which the missionary handed to him, he read in Arabic the whole chapter. "Here," said he, "is my lineage;" and added, "come with me, and I will show you that we number sixty thousand at the present day!"

Saying this he mounted his steed, and, says the missionary, flew with the swiftness of the wind, leaving behind him a standing monument of the fact that "Prophecy came not in old time by the will of man; but holy men of God spake as they were moved by the Holy Ghost." Well did Peter call it a "sure word of prophecy."

VI. With regard to the prophecies in relation to the Jews, there are none which have been more remarkably fulfilled, but they have been frequently presented; therefore, on the present occasion, I will pass over them very briefly.

It was predicted that they should be a peculiar people,—and have they not for ages and ages been a peculiar people, and are they not a peculiar people at the present time?—peculiar in their habits and manners; peculiar in their very looks? It was predicted that they should be scattered—and where is there a nation under heaven where some of this peculiar people are not found? It was predicted that they should be persecuted—only read the history of the Jews, and you will find abundant evidence that this prophecy has been fulfilled to the very letter! It was predicted that they should become a proverb and a by-word—and how common are such sayings as these: " As rich as a Jew:" and " Take care of that man, he will Jew you."

" The children of Israel shall abide many days," says the prophet, "without a king, without a prince, and without a sacrifice, and without an image, and without an ephod, and without teraphim. Afterwards shall the children of Israel return, and seek the Lord their God, and David their king, and shall fear the Lord and his goodness in the latter days." (Hosea iii. 4.) For eighteen hundred years the children of Israel have had no king, no prince, no sacrifice, no image, no ephod, no teraphim, and they now seem evidently awaiting some great event about to take place in these latter days.

I do say, that the past history of the Jews, and their present condition, furnish an evidence for the inspiration of the sacred Scriptures, which

I am bold to affirm, cannot be overturned or set aside. Young man, I repeat what I said before; your mother is right! The Bible is true! Beware how you make light of it! It will cost you your soul!

VII. One prophecy more and I have done. It is found in Daniel xii. 4. "Many shall run to and fro, and knowledge shall be increased." This prophecy is invested with peculiar interest, as I verily believe it has special reference to the times in which we live.

By reference to the context, it will be seen that the prophet speaks of the rising of an antichristian power, and that about the time of its going down "many shall run to and fro, and knowledge shall be increased."

What a mighty moving amongst the nations has there been in these latter ages! What a spirit of emigration! How they crowd in upon us from the old world! Every ship comes freighted with human beings. The tide of population flowing in upon us from all quarters of the earth is immense —something like three hundred thousand every year. And how many, in our land, are going east, west, north, and south, as business, or trade, or fancy may direct.

I am bold to say, that at this present time there is more of this running to and fro than was ever known before. Yes, literally "running."

What is now the usual mode of travelling? Is it
not in steamboats and railroad cars? And do we
not speak of one "running" ten, twelve, and
fourteen miles an hour? and the other "running"
twenty, thirty, forty, and even sixty miles an hour?
What multitudes are upon the move now, and
with what speed do they go! Surely the prophet's
mental ray was purged, and it was when he was
under the inspiration of the Almighty that he uttered
this prediction, "Many shall run to and fro;"
but this is not all, he adds, "knowledge shall be
increased."

And is there not at this time a spirit of inquiry, and a spirit of inquiry such as was never
known before? Is not the schoolmaster abroad,
and the lecturer abroad, and the missionary abroad?
It was said, "The Lord gave the word, and great
was the company of them that published it." And
so, at the present time, the Lord has willed it that
knowledge shall be increased; and how many and
varied in their characters are those who are carrying
the lights of science and religion into every land.
Old landmarks are breaking down; old prejudices
are passing away; and sacrifices are now being
kindled in every valley, and on every mountain-
top, not only throughout our boundless continent,
but even in the islands which are afar off.

This new order of things may be dated from
the period of the Reformation. Then was the

long slumber of ages broken; then was the morning-star seen to rise in splendour; and then could the great Reformers exclaim with the voice of joy and praise, " The night is far spent; the day is at hand!" Yes, congratulating each other, they might well indulge in the language of triumph and exultation, and say,

> " Christian, see the orient morning
> Breaks along the darken'd sky!
> Lo! th' expected day is dawning,
> Glorious Day-spring from on high.
>
> " Zion's Sun, salvation beaming,
> Gilding now the radiant hills,
> Rise and shine, till, brighter gleaming,
> All the world thy glory fills!"

What inventions, what discoveries, what improvements, have marked these latter ages! The invention of printing has marked a new epoch in the history of the world, and has served to spread light and increase knowledge far, very far beyond anything that our progenitors ever dreamed of. What an immense number of new books are continually coming from the press! And, as for newspapers, periodicals, and tracts of every kind, they are now being scattered over the wide world like the leaves of autumn, when the trees of the forest are swept by the mighty winds of heaven. Even children now are supplied abundantly with reading matter, rich and varied. Even so late as when I was a child, the grand total of a library for those in tender years amounted to (so far as known to me) not more than some six or eight little books; now many Sabbath-schools have at least one thousand volumes each.

The steam-power, too, what miracles has that wrought! What a new impulse has it given to printing, travelling, manufactures, and improvements of every kind! Now we are in possession of the secret of performing by one hand what required a hundred in days gone by. Moreover, we have now the blind man's book. Did our fathers ever hear of such a thing as teaching the blind to read? Our Saviour enabled the blind to see by miraculously opening their eyes; but now, without a miracle, they are taught, not to see, but to read. And is not this the increasing of knowledge in a new quarter?

But, not to enlarge, there is that "wonder of all wonders"—that great wonder of the age—the magnetic telegraph! Who ever heard of mortal man's annihilating time and space? And yet here is an invention which, to all intents and purposes, does it; for, in the conveyance of a message, there is no perceptible difference between one mile and a thousand. How astonishing is this! How it spreads knowledge, and how it proves its mighty increase!

The prophet, some twenty-five hundred years ago, referring, as we verily believe, to the very age in which we live, uttered the prophecy, " Many shall run to and fro, and knowledge shall be increased." How clear must have been the vision of him who could predict such things ! Everything was as if then passing directly and in full view before his eyes. Surely the most sceptical must now bow before the power of divine truth. Surely the most obstinate must admit that " Prophecy came not in old time by the will of man, but holy men of God spake as they were moved by the Holy Ghost."

And now, if these prophecies are true, must not all others recorded in the same sacred volume bear the same sacred character ? Permit me simply to remind you of a few : " Say ye to the righteous, it shall be well with him ; woe to the wicked, it shall be ill with him." " He that believeth and is baptized shall be saved, but he that believeth not shall be damned." " The hour cometh when all that are in their graves shall hear the voice of the Son of God, and shall come forth ; they that have done good to the resurrection of life, and they that have done evil to the resurrection of damnation." Let, then, the righteous rejoice, for heaven, with all its joys, is just at hand ! Let the sinner tremble, for hell, with all its sorrows, is not far off ! Another moment, and the Christian may be in paradise with God and his angels! Another moment, and the Christless soul may be in tophet with devils and damned spirits!

Awake, one! awake, all! for eternity is nigh, even at the door, and the night cometh, when no man can work! Let no one trifle with matters of such high import! The Bible is true, and all its declarations may assuredly be depended upon. The argument for the inspiration of the sacred volume drawn from prophecy, is only one amongst many, but is of itself convincing; and the man who is an unbeliever, in view of the evidence drawn from this source, would not believe though one rose from the dead.

Permit me, also, to guard you against infidelity. As this is a day of abounding iniquity; as intemperance, profane swearing, Sabbath-breaking, gambling, and other kindred vices, are, alas! too common in our midst, we may expect infidelity, at least in some of its forms, to keep pace with these things; for, as one well remarks, "Infidelity is a disease of the heart, not of the head." Let the morals be corrupt, and the sentiments will soon become loose. Let the heart be infected with vice, and infidelity will forthwith spring up, like green scum upon the surface of a foul and stagnant pool.

Beware of infidelity! It wars against reason

and common sense, against God and the best interests of man. Beware of infidelity! It teaches that man is not responsible to his Maker for his actions, however atrocious they may be, and that in the end it will be as well with the gambler and the pirate as with the man of virtue and religion. Beware of infidelity! It curses the body, and curses the soul; it curses you in time, and it will curse you through all eternity. Beware of infidelity! It will poison the stream of public morals, and public happiness; it will rob you of your dearest hopes and sweetest comforts; it will rob you of the favour of God; it will hang around your dying bed the curtains of gloom and despair. It will lay your body in an unblest grave, and your soul "in the urn of ever-lasting death!" I have heard the saying, "Cry Havoc, and let slip the dogs of war;" but he who encourages infidelity, in a more fearful sense cries "Havoc!" and lets slip, not the dogs of war, but the spirits of Pandemonium, and the demons of the pit!

Young man, listen to me: I repeat once more what I have said before—your Christian mother is right—the Bible is true! and if you die without the repentance which it enjoins, and the Saviour which it reveals, mark my word, in the great day of judgment you will wish that you had never been born!

CHRIST THE MEDIATOR.

––––––––––

" Who, being in the form of God, thought it not robbery to be equal with God : but made Himself of no reputation, and took upon Him the form of a servant, and was made in the likeness of men : and being found in fashion as a man, He humbled Himself and became obedient unto death, even the death of the cross. Wherefore God also hath highly exalted Him, and given Him a name which is above every name ; that at the name of Jesus. every knee should bow, of things in heaven, and things in earth, and things under the earth ; and that every tongue should 'confess that Jesus Christ is Lord, to the glory of God the Father."— PHIL. ii. 6—11.

In these words, my friends, we have,

I. The mediatorial character, work, and glory of Christ ; and

II. The grand design of the whole.

I. The mediatorial character, work, and glory of Christ.—By the mediatorial *character* of Christ, we are to understand, not his essential, but his official character—that which He, as Mediator, sustains in the economy of man's redemption.

Had man never existed; or existing, never fallen; or falling, never been redeemed, the Eternal Son of God had never assumed the name of Jesus Christ or Mediator. This is, unquestionably, that new name spoken of in the Book of Revelation (iii. 12), and that name which is above every name, made mention of in the passage now before us. Entering upon the glorious work of man's redemption, He assumes a new name, and sustains a new character. This character is commonly denominated his mediatorial character.

The scope of our text would lead us, however, to speak, not so much of those offices which belong to the mediatorial character of Christ, as of that union of the human and divine nature in the person of Christ, upon which the mediatorial character is founded, and which indeed gives to it all its dignity, and sweetness, and excellence, and perfection.

Here it will be necessary for us, by sound scriptural argument, to establish this proposition, that *Jesus Christ, as Mediator, possesses two natures—the divine and the human—in mysterious yet all harmonious union.* This is a doctrine of prime importance. It lies at the very foundation of the whole Christian system; and with it, the most precious hopes of the believer must live or die. No wonder, then, if we be tenacious for this doctrine; no wonder if we cling to it as the

miser clings to his gold; for "if the foundations
be destroyed, what can the righteous do ?"

In establishing this point, we shall adduce
only one argument, with some collateral proofs—
I say only one argument, but that, humbly con-
ceived to be, both clear and unanswerable—it is
this : In this volume, the Bible, there are certain
things affirmed of Jesus Christ, which can properly be affirmed only of the *human* nature; and
yet, in the very same volume, certain other things
are affirmed of Him which can properly be affirmed
only of the *divine* nature.   Now these two classes
of affirmations, in the very nature of the case,
cannot be true, except on the principle that Jesus
Christ possesses, as we have said, both the human
and divine nature, in mysterious yet all harmonious
union.

How do we prove that a living man possesses,
both a soul and body in union ?   Very much in
this way.   Speaking of this man, for example, I
say that he has flesh, bones, blood, and is mortal.
These things, we all see, belong not to his soul,
but to his body, and prove—what?   Certainly
that he has a true body.   Yet, speaking of the
very same individual, I change my language, and
also affirm that he has memory, will, and understanding, and is immortal.   Now here is a new
set of attributes, which evidently belong not to
the body, but to the soul, and prove—what ?

Assuredly, that this man has also a soul, a reasonable soul. The connecting link between the soul and the body may be unseen; the union may be absolutely inscrutable. It matters not, the facts are clear, and therefore the inference is irresistible: this man has, in himself, mind and matter united; he has both a soul and a body, in mysterious yet harmonious union.

Now let us bring this principle of reasoning to bear upon the case in hand. And first, with regard to the human nature of Christ. Here we need not enlarge; the doctrine is not controverted; we need only remind you of those passages of Scripture, which tell us plainly, that Jesus Christ was born of a woman; was made under the law —and that He wept, hungered, thirsted, died! These things, we all see, appertain not to the divine nature, but to the human, and prove— what? Certainly that Jesus Christ possessed the human nature; was very man, had a true body, and a reasonable soul; was as truly a man as any in this assembly. This is a precious doctrine; we have never denied it—the apostle never did— his language is this: "Forasmuch as the children were partakers of flesh and blood, He also himself likewise took part of the same."

But with regard to the second point, that in connection with the human nature our Saviour also possessed a nature strictly speaking *divine.*

Notice the affirmations in our text: " Who, being in the form of God, thought it not robbery to be equal with God." Here are two affirmations, having reference to the supreme divinity of Christ. Take the first, " Who, being in the form of God." Here, the apostle affirms that, originally, Jesus Christ was in the form of God. Now as God is an infinite Spirit, possessed of incommunicable attributes, and arrayed in peerless, uncreated glory, it is very certain that no mere creature can possess the real form of God; and that it is the real, and not assimilated form of God, is evident from what the apostle says in his Epistle to the Hebrews (i. 3), where he declares Jesus Christ to be the brightness of the Father's glory, and the express image of his person. " The brightness of His glory."

Now as the brightness of the natural sun in the heavens is of the same nature and date with that great luminary itself, and may be distinguished, but not separated, even so, in the unity of the Godhead, the Father and the Son are in essence one and the same, co-equal, co-eternal. They may be distinguished, but not separated. When, therefore, the apostle declares that Jesus Christ was in the form of God, the idea is this, that Jesus Christ possesses in Himself, really and substantially, all the perfections of God the Father's person.

In confirmation of this, notice the following remarkable facts : 1. That the sublimest works of the Supreme God are ascribed to Christ.—Is creation the work of God? No man denies it; and yet John tells us that, " All things were made by Him ; and without Him was not anything made that was made " (John i. 3). Is preservation the work of God ? Who denies that ? And yet Paul tells us that Jesus Christ upholdeth all things by the word of his power (Heb. i. 3). Is the work of resurrection the work of God? Who but an omnipotent God can wake up the slumbering nations of the dead, whose ashes have been scattered to the four winds of heaven ; buried, it may be, beneath the mountain's base and the ocean's wave? Yet the blessed Saviour says, " *I* am the resurrection and the life ; I will raise him up at the last day " (John xi. 25). Is the work of final judgment the work of God ? The Bible says expressly, God is Judge himself ; and yet the apostle says, " We must all appear before the judgment-seat of Christ " (2 Cor. v. 10).

But the doctrine before us falls in with another remarkable fact, that the sublimest names of the Supreme God are given to Jesus Christ, viz. God. Thus the Everlasting Father, addressing the Son, says, " Thy throne, O God, is for ever and ever " (Heb. i. 8). " True God ; " thus John says, " Jesus Christ, this is the true God " (1 John v. 20).

" Mighty God " (Isa. ix. 6). " The Lord of Glory "
(1 Cor. ii. 8). " The Prince of Life" (Acts iii. 15).
" The First and the Last " (Rev. ii. 8). " The
Almighty" (Rev. i. 8). " Over all, God blessed for
ever " (Rom. ix. 5). Now, give these names to
Peter, or to Paul, to Michael, to Gabriel, to the
loftiest angel in heaven, and there is blasphemy in
it ; and yet they are given to Christ, and that, too,
by those who spake as they were moved by the
Holy Ghost. This can be accounted for only by
the fact stated, that Jesus Christ possesses in
Himself, really and substantially, all the perfections
of God the Father's person.

And notice how this doctrine falls in with
another remarkable fact, that the sublimest honours
of the Supreme God are given to Jesus Christ.
Witness the language of Thomas : " My Lord,
and my God." Witness what is said of Stephen,
the first martyr : " And they stoned Stephen, calling upon God, and saying, Lord Jesus, receive my
spirit." Witness the form of baptism : " In the
name of the Father, and of the Son, and of the
Holy Ghost." Now whatever is to be implied in
the name of the Father, is of course also to be implied in the name of the Son. But hark ! pæans
are sounding in the world above ! " Worthy is the
Lamb that was slain to receive power, and riches,
and wisdom, and strength, and honour, and glory,
and blessing" (Rev. v. 12). There is no adoration

loftier than this ; no worship more, strictly speaking, divine ; yet Jesus Christ is the object of it.

What makes this matter more remarkable is this : it is written, " Thou shalt worship the Lord thy God, and Him only shalt thou serve." Accordingly, we find that no good man, no good angel, ever consented to receive divine honours. No good man. Paul and Barnabas were good men : having wrought a stupendous miracle at Lystra, the people cried out, in the language of Lycaonia, " The gods have come down to us in the likeness of men : " and the priests of Jupiter brought oxen and garlands to the gates of the city, and would have done sacrifice with the people—would have paid Paul and Barnabas divine honours. Did these good men consent ? They rent their clothes, and ran in amongst the people, crying out and saying, " Sirs ! why do ye these things ? we are men of like passions with you." No good angel ever consented to receive divine honours. You recollect a good angel once appeared to John, in the Isle of Patmos. John, dazzled by the effulgence of his splendour, fell down at his feet to worship him. Did this good angel consent to receive this divine honour ? He was in haste to repel it ; "I am thy fellow-servant—worship God." See then, how good men and angels all point to Supreme divinity as the only proper object of religious worship and adoration.

Now, is it not remarkable that the blessed . Saviour himself appeared to the same John, in the same Isle of Patmos, and John, dazzled by the effulgence of his splendour, fell down at his feet also? Did He then give the holy apostle any charge against worshipping *Him?* Mark the difference! He laid his right hand upon him, saying, " Fear not, I am the First and the Last! I am He that liveth, and was dead, and behold I am alive for evermore, amen ; and have the keys of hell and of death!" And this reminds me of that sublime doxology uttered by the same exile in Patmos, in his own name and that of the whole church, militant and triumphant—" Unto Him that loved us, and washed us from our sins in his own blood, and hath made us kings and priests unto God and his Father ; to Him be glory and dominion, for ever and ever." Mark, " to *Him* who loved us and washed us from our sins in his own blood—to *Him* be glory and dominion, for ever and ever." Let any being be invested with glory and dominion for ever and ever, and he is invested with the honours of Supreme divinity—he ascends the throne of the universe, and he is inaugurated God over all.

These things, in relation to Jesus Christ, are very remarkable, and can be explained, as I humbly conceive, only on the ground already stated, that Jesus Christ possesses in Himself, real and substantially, all the perfections of God the Father's person. In confirmation of this position, take this passage of Scripture : " Philip saith unto Him, Lord, show us the Father, and it sufficeth us. Jesus saith unto him, Have I been so long time with you, and yet hast thou not known Me, Philip ? He that hath seen *Me* hath seen the *Father :* and how sayest thou then, Show us the Father ? Believest thou not that I am in the Father, and the Father in Me ? " (John xiv. 8, 9, 10). To crown the matter, notice how the apostle expresses the doctrine almost in the very words which we have uttered : " In Him (Jesus Christ) dwelleth all the fulness of the Godhead bodily " (Col. ii. 9). How strong is this language ! Every word emphatic ! In Him, Jesus Christ, dwelleth all the fulness of the Godhead bodily. If this does not express the idea of God incarnate—literally God *incarnate* —what idea does it present ? And here I would remark—as thought, written or uttered, is thought embodied; so Christ, in human form, is God made manifest in the flesh.

Having introduced the term " Godhead," permit me to make a [remark or two touching the mysterious and sublime doctrine of the Trinity. Some stumble at it, but why ? According to philosophers, and, what is incomparably better, according to the Scripture, man himself, who is said to have been made after the similitude of

God—yes, man himself consists of three distinc-
tions : spirit, soul, and body, (1 Thess. v. 23). By
the body, we understand the material frame ; by
the soul, the animal life, which we have, in common with the brutes that perish ; and by the spirit
(usually called the soul), the immortal principle.
Now here, we perceive, even in ourselves, according to this statement, a threefold existence, not
only in union, but in unity. Why, then, should
we stumble at the doctrine of the Trinity as revealed in the sacred volume ? The truth is, in
our catechisms, creeds, and confessions, the doctrine of the Trinity is presented, if I may so speak,
in a skeleton form, and therefore presented to
great disadvantage, for no *skeleton* has any charms ;
but in the sacred volume it is presented in living
beauty, each person in the adorable Godhead being
there presented as sustaining some peculiar office
in the economy of redemption. For example :
the Father is represented as planning the glorious
scheme of man's redemption ; the Son as exe-
cuting that scheme ; and the Holy Ghost, as ap-
plying to all believers the benefits of that planned
and purchased redemption, and thus exhibiting the
Godhead to a ruined world, in glorious, yet dis-
tinct manifestations.

But to resume the argument touching the
supreme divinity of Christ : We have shown that
Jesus Christ, as Mediator, possesses two natures,

the divine and human, in mysterious, yet all-har-
monious union. Ah! this *mysterious* union!
Some stumble at the *mystery* of the incarnation;
and is not the union of soul and body in man a
mystery? and yet who stumbles at this? Having
evidence of the fact, we believe the one; why not,
having evidence of the fact, believe the other also?
But was the apostle Paul aware of the mystery?
He was. Did *he* stumble at it? I give you his
own words, you can judge as well as I. " Without controversy," says he, " great is the mystery
of godliness. God was manifest in the flesh "
(1 Tim. iii. 6). Observe: he admits it to be a
mystery — he goes farther; he admits it to be a
great mystery; moreover, he would have us to understand, that there is no use to have any controversy upon this point. The mystery of the
incarnation is not denied. " Without controversy,
great is the mystery of godliness. God was manifest in the flesh." Now, if the apostle did not
stumble at the mystery of the human and divine
nature in the person of Christ, neither do I—nay,
more, he gloried in it, (Rom. ix. 5); and therefore
so will I. And, indeed, well may we all; for, as
I shall now show you, if it be a mystery, it is a
blessed mystery—full of sweetness as well as full
of wonder; for, observe—

1. How essential the twofold nature of Christ
is to the various parts of his mediatorial work.

For example, He must have a human nature to obey the law which man had violated, and thus to magnify the law and make it honourable ; but it is equally necessary, in this matter, that He should have a Divine nature also to give merit to his obedience.

Suppose that Jesus Christ were a mere man, what could his obedience avail ? He would have to say, as we do, I am an unprofitable servant; I have done no more than was my duty; but, according to the Scriptures, by his obedience shall many be made righteous. So He must have a human nature to obey the law, and the Divine nature to stamp value upon that obedience.

Again, He must have a human nature to suffer, and the Divine nature to give efficacy to those sufferings. Yes, according to the Scriptures, the Mediator must suffer, as it is written, " He must suffer many things of the elders, and chief priests, and scribes, and be killed, and the third day rise again " (Matt. xvi. 21). And again, " It behoved Christ to suffer " (Luke xxiv. 46). And again, " Ought not Christ to have suffered these things ?" (Luke xxiv. 26). Nay more, it is written, " Without the shedding of blood there is no remission " (Heb. ix. 22). In order to make an atonement, then, Christ must become a substitutionary sacrifice—must suffer; but the Divine nature cannot suffer, cannot be wounded for our transgressions, nor bruised for our iniquities. Hence, Christ must have a human nature to suffer; but here again it is equally necessary that He should have a Divine nature, as we have stated, to give efficacy to his sufferings, for, suppose Jesus Christ were no more than a mere man, what could his sufferings avail? The martyrs suffered much, their blood flowed in torrents! but we never hear that the blood of the martyrs availed to the washing away of a single sin of their own; but with regard to this mysterious sufferer it is said, "His blood cleanseth from all sin" (1 John i. 7). And again, "Behold the Lamb of God, which taketh away the sin of the world!" (John i. 29).

Thus you perceive it is necessary that Jesus Christ, as Mediator, should possess a human nature to suffer, and also a Divine nature to give efficacy to those sufferings. But some man may say, "Sir, you have thrown some light upon this point, but the point is not clear yet. You say that the human nature cannot merit, nor the Divine nature suffer, then, after all, how can the sufferings of the human nature of Christ have so much efficacy?" I reply, there is no difficulty here at all. Here is a clod of earth. In that form you may strike it about at pleasure—no harm done; but let this clod of earth be formed into the body of a man; let it be united to the soul of a man, a prince, a king, a conqueror! and, verily, you may not now strike it about at your pleasure! Who does not see that an injury done to that clod of earth, in its new form, as united to the soul of a man, a prince, a king, a conqueror, is, to all intents and purposes, the same as an injury done to the soul of that man, that prince, that king, that conqueror? The case, then, is simply this, although the human nature of Christ could not merit nor his Divine nature suffer, yet, by virtue of the union of the human and Divine nature in the person of Christ, the sufferings of the human are as if they were the sufferings of the Divine nature. "It is the altar which sanctifies the gift." The Saviour himself furnishes the illustration. The Divine nature is the altar, the human nature of Christ is the victim offered upon that altar, and the altar sanctifies the gift—the very illustration of Christ himself!

But again, Christ, as Mediator, must have a human nature to have a brother's heart; a Divine nature to have an almighty arm. You recollect that when God descended, in terrible majesty, upon Sinai's awful mount, the people, greatly alarmed, removed and stood afar off, and said unto Moses, "Speak thou with us, and we will hear; but let not God speak with us, lest we die." Nay, even Moses himself exclaimed, "I do exceedingly fear and quake!" How natural then to wish, with the man of Uz, that there were some days-man to lay his hand upon both parties. In our blessed Redeemer this desire is fully met, for, as we have said, He has a human nature to have a brother's heart, a Divine nature to have an almighty arm. Both natures are equally necessary, for suppose that Christ had a human nature only, then certainly He could have a brother's heart, could sympathize with us, being touched with a fellow feeling of our infirmities, and this would be soothing; but if this were all, amid all his tender sympathies, we might sink down in hopeless sorrow. But, oh, delightful truth! our Mediator is, in all respects, fitted for his appointment. As a man He has all the innocent sensibilities of our nature—

> "He knows what sore temptations mean,
> For He has felt the same."

"We have not an High Priest," says the apostle, "who cannot be touched with a feeling of our infirmities, but was tempted in all points like as we are, yet without sin." Yes, it is even so:—

> "He, in the days of feeble flesh,
> Poured out his cries and tears;
> And in his measure feels afresh
> What every member bears."

This is a precious doctrine. The human nature of Christ brings Him very near to our hearts, and the idea, that, exalted as He is, He can be touched with a fellow feeling of our infirmities, is, I repeat it, very soothing; but if this were all, what would it avail to the saving of our souls? No! He must have something more than sympathy, He must have power. He must have something more than a brother's heart, He must have an almighty arm; and, according to our doctrine, so it is; hence, in the Scriptures, He is presented to us as one able to save unto the uttermost (Heb. vii. 25).

O glorious Mediator! O precious Redeemer! One who has all the glories of a God, attempered with the milder beauties of a perfect man! One so distant, and yet so near! Only think, my brethren (sweet thought!) our blessed Saviour has a human nature, to have a brother's heart!—a divine nature, to have an almighty arm!

> " Till God in human flesh I see,
>   My thoughts no comfort find ;
> The Holy, Just, and Sacred Three,
>   Are terrors to my mind ;
>
> But if Immanuel's face appear,
>   My hope, my joy begins ;
> His name forbids my slavish fear,
>   His grace removes my sins.
>
> While Jews on their own law rely,
>   And Greeks of wisdom boast,
> I love th' incarnate mystery,
>   And there I fix my trust."

If the twofold nature of Christ be a mystery (and I deny it not), it is a blessed mystery, full of

sweetness as well as full of wonder; for, observe—

2. How beautifully it falls in with the account
given of our blessed Saviour, whilst He tabernacled
here on earth. In this account, circumstances of
humility, and circumstances of grandeur, are made
strangely and sweetly to blend together in the person of Christ; pointing out, at the same time,
both his *human* and *divine* nature. See the
blessed Saviour, born in Bethlehem; born of a
woman, and laid in a manger ! Here are circumstances of humility, pointing out his *human*
nature; but mark the circumstances of grandeur
proclaiming his divine nature. A star announces
his birth, and angels sing his natal song ! Sec
Him at the grave of Lazarus ! He weeps *like a
man;* and then, with authority, says, " Lazarus,
come forth ! " *like a God.* Approaching the
barren fig-tree, He hungers *like a man ;* and then,
like a God, causes it, by his word, to wither away.
During a raging storm on the sea of Tiberias, He
lay in the hinder part of the ship, with his head
upon a pillow ; He slept *like a man.* Being called
upon, He arose and rebuked the winds and the
sea, *like a God.* Having wrought a stupendous
miracle, He goes into a mountain apart to pray,
like a man ; and at the fourth watch of the night,
He comes to his disciples, walking upon the water,
like a God. *As a man,* He pays tribute money ;

as a God, He causes a fish of the deep to bring to
Him the tribute money.   Disciples of Christ! oh
see your Saviour on yonder bloody tree! nailed to
the cross, He suffers *like a man;* and yet, in the
midst of his sufferings, He opens the gates of
Paradise to the dying thief, *like a God.*   And see,
too, in yonder sepulchre, alas! in yonder sepulchre
—the hope of Israel, wrapt in the winding-sheet,
lies, pale and cold in death, *like a man.*   But lo!
in the morning of the third day, by his own immortal energies, He bursts the bands of death, and
arises triumphant, *like a God!*   And see Him, too,
after his resurrection : He meets with his disciples, takes a piece of a broiled fish, and of an
honeycomb, and eats with them, *like a man;*
And then He leads them out to Bethany and
blesses them; and as He blesses them, He
ascends in a cloud in radiant majesty, far above
all heavens, *a God confessed!*   "God is gone up
with a shout!   The Lord with the sound of a
trumpet!   Sing praises unto God; sing praises!
Sing praises unto our King; sing praises!"

> " All hail the power of Jesu's name,
>   Let angels prostrate fall ;
>   Bring forth the royal diadem,
>   And crown Him Lord of all."

3. If the union of the human and divine
nature in the person of Christ be a mystery, it is

a blessed mystery, for it serves very clearly and beautifully to harmonize many passages of Scripture which, on no other principle, I verily believe, can be made to harmonize.

For example: In one place Jesus Christ is called a man; in another place, God (Heb. i. 8). In one place, David's Son (Matt. xxii. 42); in another place, David's Lord (Matt. xxii. 45). In one place He says, "My Father is greater than I" (John x. 29); in another place, "I and my Father are one" (John x. 30). In one place He is said to be a Lamb slain; in another place, the Prince of Life, who only hath immortality.* Now deny our doctrine, and I defy any man on earth, or angel in heaven, to reconcile these passages. Admit the doctrine, and all is beautiful and harmonious. With regard to his *human* nature, Jesus Christ is a *man;* with regard to his *divine* nature, *God:* with regard to his *human* nature, He is David's Son; with regard to his *divine* nature, David's Lord. Referring to his *human* nature, or official character, He can say, "My Father is greater than I;" referring to his *divine* nature, or essential character, He can say, "I and my Father are one." As to his *human* nature, He is a *Lamb slain;* as to his *divine* nature, the *Prince of Life,* who only hath immortality.

And now, to put the beauteous crown upon

* Compare Acts iii. 15; Rev. xix. 16; 1 Tim. vi. 15, 16.

the whole, and to convince you that this is indeed
the true Scriptural doctrine, hear the words of the
Saviour himself : " I am the root and offspring of
David, and the bright and morning star." Now,
this is a very remarkable passage of Scripture, and
should settle the doctrine of the twofold nature
of Christ for ever; for, observe, if Jesus Christ
possessed the divine nature, and that only, He
could most assuredly be David's root, the source
of David's being. But in this case, how could
He be David's offspring ? On the other hand, if
Jesus Christ possessed the human nature, and
that only, He could then certainly be David's
offspring; but here, again, how, in this case,
could He be David's root, the source of David's
being ? But possessing both the human and
divine nature, He can say, as He does say, " I
am the root and offspring of David, and the bright
and morning star;" evidently referring to his
mediatorial character. "Rising," as one remarks,
" in his incarnation, as the bright and morning
star, He introduced the gospel day; rising as the
bright and morning star in the influences of his
Spirit, He introduces the day of grace and comfort in the sinner's soul; and rising, at last, in his
bright appearing to judge the world, He will to his
saints usher in the coronation-day—the day of a
blest eternity. Bright and morning Star ! Star
of hope to the dying sinner ! Star of hope to a

sinking world! Oh, shine upon this heart of mine!

Having considered the mediatorial character of Christ, let us next consider his mediatorial work. And by this we are to understand all that our blessed Saviour did, and suffered, to achieve the redemption of man, commonly termed his active and passive obedience. It would very far transcend the limits of this discourse to lay before you in detail all the varied parts of the mediatorial work of Christ; nor is it necessary on the present occasion, for, by a very common figure of speech, a part is here put for the whole—the apostle summing up the whole in the humiliation of Christ; and this, with singular propriety, in the connection of our text, inasmuch as his deep humiliation on earth is here presented in striking contrast with the august dignity which He originally had, when, being in the form of God, He thought it not robbery to be equal with God. In this astonishing humiliation there are several steps.

1. "He was made in the likeness of men." That is, He, who originally "was the brightness of the Father's glory, and the express image of his person," was, in his incarnation, so veiled, so clouded, that He no longer appeared in the form of God, but in the likeness of men. " Forasmuch as the children were partakers of flesh and blood,"

says the apostle, "He also Himself took part of
the same." What a stoop of condescension!
The Prince of Life and Lord of Glory, in the likeness of men!

2. "He took upon Him the form of a servant."
Observe! This glorious One not only took upon
Him human nature, but human nature in a low
condition: "He took upon Him," says our text,
"the form of a servant;" not the form of a prince
or a king, but the form of a servant. How wonderful is this! Nor was He ashamed to take this
step of humiliation for the good of man; He
rather gloried in it; and how touching are his
allusions to this very thing! "The Son of Man,"
says He, "came not to be ministered unto, but to
minister;" that is, to act the part of a servant.
And again said He to his disciples, "Whether is
greater, he that sitteth at meat, or he that serveth?
Is not he that sitteth at meat? but I am among
you as he that serveth." Blessed Jesus! But
most emphatically did our great Redeemer assume
the form of a servant, when, rising from the
paschal supper, He laid aside his garment, and
took a towel and girded Himself, and having
poured water into a basin, He began to wash his
disciples' feet with water, and to wipe them with
the towel wherewith He was girded.

And this is the Saviour that made my mother
sing in death!—the same Jesus, who, as thousands

have testified, "can make a dying bed feel soft as downy pillows are." Sinner! this is the Saviour whom you neglect! Is this thy kindness to thy Friend?

3. "He made Himself of no reputation." Even some servants have a high character, and are greatly esteemed, but the Lord of glory, in his mysterious incarnation, voluntarily places Himself in those circumstances in which He received not the honours due to his name. "He came unto his own," says the apostle, "and his own received Him not." Although He was the Rose of Sharon, and the Lily of the valleys yet He was esteemed as a root out of a dry ground, having no form nor comeliness; nay, more, as predicted of Him, He was "despised and rejected of men; a man of sorrows and acquainted with grief."

Oh! tell me, did not our blessed Saviour appear as one without reputation when the Samaritans refused to receive Him into their villages? when the Gadarenes besought Him to depart out of their coast? and when the men of his own city, Nazareth, led Him to the brow of the hill upon which their city was built, to cast Him down headlong, as one unfit to live?

Oh! tell me, did not the Saviour of lost men appear as one without reputation, when He was openly rejected by the chief priests and Pharisees, and reproachfully called a gluttonous man and a wine-bibber, a friend of publicans and sinners? when He was betrayed by one disciple, denied by another, and forsaken by all? when the multitude came out against Him, as against a thief, with swords and staves, to take Him? See Him arrested as a prisoner; bound as a culprit; hurried to the hall of Caiaphas; taken to Pilate's judgment bar; sent to Herod; mocked by the soldiers; crowned with thorns; arrayed in a gorgeous robe, and then sent back to Pilate again. Oh, see Him at Pilate's bar! False witnesses rise up against Him!—none dare appear in his behalf! The hall, the court, the very heavens ring with the cry, "Crucify Him! crucify Him!" A prisoner must needs be released at the feast, and Barabbas is preferred! Oh, my soul! think upon this!—Barabbas, a robber, was preferred to the blessed Jesus! Barabbas, a murderer, to the spotless Son of God!

And now, He is condemned! not by the voice of law, but by the clamour of popular fury. Pilate, it is true, calls for water, and washing his hands in the presence of the people, says, "I am innocent of the blood of this just man," yet gives Him over into the hands of his enemies! And now what a scene of still deeper humiliation is presented! The blessed Saviour is blindfolded! He is smitten upon the cheek! He is spitted upon! He is buffeted! He is scourged!—only think, scourged! And this is the One, who, according to the Scriptures, shall hereafter be seen coming in the clouds of heaven, with power and great glory! Oh the strength of a Saviour's love! how astonishing does it appear when measured by the humiliation to which He submitted for our sakes. He made Himself of no reputation! But there is yet another step of still deeper humiliation stated in our text.

4. "He humbled himself and became obedient unto death, even the death of the cross!" That the Prince of Life, and Lord of Glory, should die any death, however easy and honourable, is past all comprehension. But such a death!—the death of the cross! Oh, sinner! you know not the strength of a Saviour's love—you know not the tenderness of the dear Redeemer's heart! He died for you! died on the cross for you! and yet you slight Him every day—turn your back upon Him, and even trample under foot his precious blood! Hard-hearted, iron-hearted sinner! how could you serve your loving, dying Saviour so? "Hearts of stone, relent! relent!"—"Father, forgive them, they know not what they do!"

Having considered the mediatorial character and work of Christ, we are next to contemplate his mediatorial glory. By the mediatorial glory of Christ, we are to understand all that our blessed Redeemer receives, in his two-fold nature, as the reward of his mediatorial work. To this there is a reference in the fifty-third chapter of Isaiah ; and upon this the apostle delights to expatiate. His language here is beautiful and sublime: " Wherefore God also " (that is, the Father) " hath highly exalted Him, and given Him a name, which is above every name, that at the name of Jesus every knee should bow ; of things in heaven and things in earth, and things under the earth, and that every tongue should confess that Jesus Christ is Lord." Here the mediatorial glory of Christ is made to consist in two things, honour and dominion.

1. In Honour.—in his having a name which is above every name, the name of JESUS; the sweetest, the most charming name that men or angels ever heard ! Verily, " 'Tis music in the sinner's ears, 'tis life, and joy, and peace ! " Oh ! the sweetness of the name of Jesus, as it comes over the young convert with the power of a charm, bringing hope and comfort to his burdened soul ! Oh ! the sweetness of the name of Jesus, as it falls, like the music of heaven, upon the ear of the dying saint, enabling him to smile in death ; and, in the full hope of glory, to shout, "O death ! where is thy sting ? O grave ! where is thy victory ? "

> " Oh could I speak the matchless worth,
>   Oh could I sound the glories forth,
>   Which in my Saviour shine ;
>   I'd soar, and touch the heavenly strings,
>   And vie with Gabriel while he sings,
>   In notes almost divine !

> " I'd sing the precious blood He spilt,
> My ransom from the dreadful guilt,
> Of sin, and wrath divine ;
> I'd sing his glorious righteousness
> In which all perfect, heavenly dress,
> My soul shall ever shine ! "

But the mediatorial glory of Christ consists also—

2. In Dominion.—Yes, having finished the great work of atonement, and having ascended up on high, our great Redeemer is now, according to the Scriptures, exalted " far above all principality, and power, and might, and dominion, and every name that is named, not only in this world, but also in that which is to come " (Eph. i. 21) " He is Lord of all " (Acts x. 36). He it is, who, walking in the midst of the golden candle-sticks, holds the ministers as stars in his right hand; He it is, who, seated in the highest heavens, rules the church, and rules the world; and He it is, who, hereafter, " In that great day, for which all other days were made," shall sit as Judge of quick and dead. " Behold, He cometh with clouds," says the apostle, " and every eye shall see Him, and they also which pierced Him; and all kindreds of the earth shall wail because of Him. Even so, Amen." Yes, " hereafter "— and mark, this is his own language—" here-after, shall ye see the Son of man coming in the clouds of heaven, with power and great glory."

(Matt. xxiv. 30; xxvi. 64). Although He shall
come as the Son of man, "clothed in a body
like our own," yet, verily, none shall be able to
think lightly of Him then; for He shall come
with great power and glory—shall be revealed
from heaven, with his mighty angels, in flaming
fire.   In view of this, I would now say to every
impenitent sinner present, in the language of the
Psalmist, "Kiss the Son, lest He be angry, and ye
perish from the way, when his wrath is kindled
but a little; blessed are all they who put their
trust in Him."   But it is time to consider,

II. The grand design of the whole, beautifully
and comprehensively expressed by the apostle in
these words—"To the glory of God the Father."
On this part of our subject we shall be brief.   The
heavens, in all their varied beauties, in all their
wide and boundless magnificence, proclaim the
glory of God—proclaim his wisdom, his grandeur,
and his power; but believe me, brethren, we have
something here, which "outshines the wonders of
the skies;" something which gives a development
of the divine character to be found nowhere else.
Yes, the great scheme of man's redemption is
now, and ever will be, to the Lord emphatically
for a crown of glory, and for a diadem of beauty.
For example—

It will be to the Lord a bright and imperish-
able monument of his *love.*   "God so loved the

world," says the Saviour, " that He gave his only
begotten Son, that whosoever believeth in Him
should not perish, but have everlasting life."
Yonder sun in the heavens is exceedingly bright;
but God could have made it brighter still! The
universe is astonishingly great, but God could
have made it greater still! But is there, can
there be, any greater gift which the infinite God
himself can bestow, than the gift of his Son?
Hence the peculiar language of the Saviour—
" God *so* loved the world;" and hence also the
language of the apostle John—" Herein is love,
not that we loved God, but that He loved us, and
sent his Son to be the propitiation for our sins."

It will be to the Lord a bright and imperish-
able monument of his power, for it will appear
that it was in this way He destroyed the works of
the devil, subdued the enemies of his government,
conquered rebellious wills, softened hearts of rock,
and thus redeemed and disenthralled a guilty and
a ruined world!

It will be to the Lord a bright and imperish-
able monument of his justice. If God spared not
his own Son, when He was found in the law's
place and stead of the sinner, will He spare any
sinner who has to answer for himself? Justice
of heaven! how inflexible dost thou appear when
thy glittering sword is seen bathed in the blood
of the Son of God!

A few inferences, and I have done.

1. Here we have an unanswerable argument for the truth of the Christian religion—a doctrine such as we have now been considering; a doctrine of such mingled sweetness and grandeur, so worthy of God, and so suited to man; such a doctrine, if unrevealed, I firmly believe, could never have entered the mind of man. Woe to the infidel, he must meet a fiery day!

2. How invaluable must the soul of man be! To create worlds and systems required no great array of means. "God spake and it was done! He commanded, and it stood fast;" but, to redeem the soul of man, all heaven must be moved! The Lord of angels must become incarnate, must suffer, and bleed, and agonize, and die. In other words, there must be a mighty draft, not upon the resources of nature, but upon the resources of nature's God.

3. How dreadful is the guilt, and how terrible must be the doom of those who reject such a Saviour!—They reject whom? A dying Saviour, who is God's eternal Son! They reject whom? The world's last and only hope! There is salvation in none else; and, the sinner, dying without an interest in this Saviour, is accursed for ever! He is turned over to wrath and despair! He sinks down in the deep grave of sorrow, and no angel voice, no resurrection trump, shall wake him

up to hope and joy, any more! O sinner! sinner! You have rejected this Saviour already too long. Oh! be entreated to reject Him no more. Submit now. This may be your last call, your last day!

4. How great will be the happiness of the redeemed in heaven!—After such preparation, and such cost, to bring them to that blessed world above, how dear, oh how precious, will they be in the eyes of Him who brought them there! How will He beautify them with salvation! How will He pour into their souls the full tide of heavenly and never-ending joy! "Eye hath not seen, nor ear heard, neither have entered into the heart of man, the things which God hath prepared for them that love Him."

O heaven! sweet heaven! The dwelling-place of love and joy! the purchase of a Saviour's blood! the Christian's rest, the pilgrim's home! O heaven, sweet heaven! There rolls the river of pleasure! there flourishes the tree of life! there saints and angels mingling their splendours, have one continued festival, one never-ending jubilee! "Visions of glory! how ye crowd upon my aching sight!" "Praise God from the heavens; praise Him in the heights. Praise ye Him, all his angels; praise ye Him, all his hosts. Praise ye Him, sun and moon; praise Him, all ye stars of light. Praise ye Him, ye heavens of heavens, and ye waters that be above the heavens.   Let them praise the name of the Lord.   Praise the Lord from the earth, ye dragons, and all deeps.   Fire, and hail, and snow, and vapour, and stormy wind fulfilling his word. Mountains, and all hills; fruitful trees, and all cedars ; beasts, and all cattle; creeping things, and flying fowl; kings of the earth, and all people; princes, and all judges of the earth; both young men and maidens, old men and children; let them praise the Lord; for his name alone is excellent, his glory is above the earth and heaven. Praise God in his sanctuary; praise Him in the firmament of his power ; praise Him for his mighty acts ; praise Him according to his excellent greatness ; praise Him with the sound of the trumpet ; praise Him with the psaltery and harp; praise Him with the timbrel and dance ; praise Him with stringed instruments and organs; praise Him upon the loud cymbals, praise Him upon the high-sounding cymbals.   Let everything that hath breath praise the Lord !   Praise the Lord, O my soul ! "

NAAMAN.

"Are not Abana and Pharpar, rivers of Damascus, better than all the waters of Israel? May I not wash in them and be clean? So he turned and went away in a rage."—2 KINGS v. 12.

THE account given of Naaman in this chapter is truly interesting and instructive. It furnishes an exact delineation of the human character, and is a complete development of the pride and carnality of the natural or unrenewed man.

Naaman was a great man, in the popular sense of that term. He had been raised to a high military station, and had justified the confidence reposed in him. Leading forth the hosts of the king of Syria, he marched against the enemies of his country. He was victorious, and returned to Syria crowned with laurels, and greeted with the acclamations of his grateful countrymen. The king himself honoured him, and he was acknowledged by all as the political saviour of his country, because that "by him the Lord had given deliver-

ance to Syria." Crowned with laurels and enriched with spoils, he stood upon a proud eminence,
the boast of his country, the admiration of all!

Yet there was one thing against him—one
thing to humble the pride of his heart—he was a
leper. This leprosy was a loathsome disease. It
was a certain breaking out upon the body, and
was of such a nature as to mar the beauty of the
person, and to make him an object of loathing to
those around, insomuch that, by a law of Moses,
the leper was required to be separated from the
congregation as unclean, unfit to mingle with
society; and we find that this law was rigidly
enforced in every instance of leprosy. The highest
characters in the nation were not exempted from
its operation. Hence you may recollect that when
king Uzziah was smitten with leprosy in the house
of the Lord, he was not only put out of the house
of the Lord, but was driven from his palace;
made to inhabit a separate house; and when he
died he was not buried in the royal sepulchre, but
in a certain field belonging to the kings, because
he was a leper!

This being the case, we may well suppose that
few wished to be Naaman, with all his wealth, his
splendour, and renown. Indeed, the Syrian conqueror would, no doubt, himself most willingly
have exchanged a palace for a cottage, could he
only in this way have been delivered from the

leprosy which cleaved to him. Whilst you see Naaman seated under a gilded canopy, amid all the insignia of wealth and honour, perhaps no other feelings are awakened in your bosom than those of loathing and disgust. You would not be a Naaman, with all his pomp, with all his riches, and with all his renown—and why? Because he is a leper!

But now, whilst you turn away from a leprous Naaman—whilst your very heart sickens at the thought of his impurities—oh; tell me, may there not be some here covered with a leprosy of a more loathsome, more dangerous kind? I mean the leprosy of sin. And what though this leprosy should not cut off the leper from the congregation and society here below, mark my word, if uncleansed, it must, it will cut him off from a better congregation and a more glorious society in a better world than this, for

" Those holy gates for ever bar
    Pollution, sin, and shame ;
None shall obtain admittance there
    But followers of the Lamb."

In speaking further from the words of our text, I wish to notice some points of resemblance between a leprous Naaman and an awakened sinner ; and I am free to say, I do think that the points of resemblance are very exact.

I. *Both are diseased.*—Naaman was a leper, so

also is the sinner; and although the leprosy of the one was of a natural or physical character, and the leprosy of the other moral or spiritual, yet in several particulars they strongly resemble each other.

Was the leprosy of Naaman polluting? So also is the leprosy of sin. Indeed, there is nothing more polluting than sin. It mars all beauty, and makes the subject thereof loathsome and abominable in the sight of a pure and holy God. Hence the language of Isaiah, "Woe is me, for I am undone, for I am a man of unclean lips, and I dwell in the midst of a people of unclean lips; for mine eyes have seen the King, the Lord of hosts." And hence, also, the language of the man of Uz, "I have heard of thee by the hearing of the ear, but now mine eye seeth thee, wherefore I abhor myself, and repent in dust and ashes."

Was the leprosy of Naaman destructive of happiness? There is nothing in all the universe more destructive of all happiness than sin. It is that which has ruined angels and ruined man! It is that which has occasioned every tear of sorrow, every sigh of grief, and every pang of agony! It is that which has withered everything that is fair, blasted everything that is good, and made bitter everything that is sweet! It is that which has dried up every spring of comfort, and rolled a tide of sorrow far and wide!

Was the leprosy of Naaman a deadly disease, not to be cured by any mortal power? So, also, is the leprosy of sin. It strikes its roots deep into the centre of the soul, generates therein a worm which shall never die, and kindles therein a fire never to be quenched. It spreads disease and death over the whole moral man! Yes, and the awakened sinner is sensible of his spiritual maladies. He remembers the words of the prophet, " The whole head is sick; the whole heart is faint. From the sole of the foot, even unto the head, there is no soundness in it, but wounds, and bruises, and putrefying sores." The understanding is darkened, the heart is hard, the will rebellious, and the conscience seared. Everything is wrong! There is a deep and total depravity! If there be some good affections, they are mixed up with sin; if some amiable traits of character, they are like blocks of marble, and beautiful columns in a house not plumb; or, like the mechanism of a watch which has been magnetized, and therefore not fit for use. Something must be done! There must be some renovating process—ay, and something accomplished by a Divine power—or the sinner's case is hopeless. He is ruined and undone for ever! But this leads me to remark—

II. *Both Naaman and the awakened sinner are miserable.* They have trouble and distress—really can enjoy nothing. Naaman, crowned with laurels, and enriched with spoils, wanted nothing, it seems, to make him happy but a healthful and vigorous body. Wanting this, the man is wretched. Ah! what is all the pomp of royalty, what all the splendour of wealth and the delicacy of viands, to one unfitted to enjoy them? Even so it is with the awakened sinner. It may be fair and serene without; it is not so within, for the wicked are as the troubled sea which cannot rest, whose waters cast up mire and dirt. A sudden death alarms him; awful dispensations of Providence force painful convictions upon his mind; or, perchance, conflicting passions rage within, and make him wretched.

Now, too, it may be, the sunshine of prosperity is darkened; the clouds of adversity are lowering around. The sinner feels, or thinks he feels, the mud-walled cottage trembling, breaking down, and, alas! for him, he has no building of God; no house made without hands, eternal, and on high! And now, also, it may be, conscience wakes to sleep no more. Remorse for the past throws his thoughts upon the future; worse dread of the future strikes them back upon the past! He turns, and turns, and finds no ray. Does the clock strike, he is ready to cry out with the despairing, dying Altamont: " O time! time! it is fit that thou shouldst thus strike thy murderer to the heart! How art thou fled for ever! A month, a day; I ask not for years, though an age were too little for the much which I have to do!"

Or say, he is no despairing, dying Altamont— is he an awakened sinner? he is not at rest—he is not happy—he cannot be! In the possession of riches, of honours, of "all the world calls good or great," "his heart distrustful asks, if this be joy?" There is a burden upon his soul, the burden of sin—a burden too heavy for him to bear. Amid the pursuits of the day his mind is thoughtful; amid the shades of the night his eyes are wakeful. He sighs. He groans inwardly. He knows not what to do. He knows not where to turn—is ready to ask, What must I do? Is ready to cry out, "God be merciful to me a sinner!"

Oh yes, the awakened sinner is not happy; he is miserable; he feels wretched. He is, perhaps, almost ready to wish he had never been born. He feels that he is a sinner, and knows not how to get rid of his sins. He knows he must die, and his conscience tells him that he is not prepared to die. He believes that after death comes the judgment, and, alas! what will become of him in the judgment day? He is ready toexclaim, Oh that I were a Christian! I would give the world only to have the Christian's hope! This leads me to notice another point of resemblance between a leprous Naaman and an awakened sinner.

III. *Both are willing to go far and do much to*

obtain a cure—are willing to do anything, if they can only obtain the object desired, *in their own way.* To be delivered from this leprosy, Naaman was willing, for a season, to withdraw from the splendours of a court, the adulations of his flatterers, and the caresses of his countrymen : he was willing to come all the way from Syria to Samaria— moreover, he was willing to give ten talents of silver, six thousand pieces of gold, and ten changes of raiment; nay, he was willing to do almost anything in the world, if by that means he could get rid of the leprosy which cleaved to him.

Just so it is with the awakened sinner; he is willing to go far and do much to obtain salvation. If he were required to perform penances, or go on a pilgrimage to Mecca, or brave the fury and storm of battle;—if he were required to bestow all his goods to feed the poor, and give his body to be burned—or leap down the Falls of Niagara, to secure salvation, I believe he would willingly do it !—anything, if he can only be permitted to have his own way, and purchase salvation.

Oh, how the awakened sinner does long to ride to heaven in a chariot of his own! How he does long to wash his robes, and make them white by the labour of his own hands! A legal spirit is deeply seated in his bosom. It is a part of his unrenewed nature; hence, every sinner, when awakened, immediately goes about to work out his own righteousness. He goes from duty to duty, from ordinance to ordinance, from resolution to resolution; thus endeavouring to establish a righteousness of his own. Forgetting the words of the apostle, " By grace are ye saved, through faith, and that not of yourselves, it is the gift of God: not of works, lest any man should boast:" forgetting, I say, all this, he labours hard to merit salvation, and thus be his own saviour.

But, as a person may go one hundred leagues, and not reach a place only one mile distant— because he does not go in the right way—so many a sinner, greatly desiring to obtain salvation, has done much to obtain it, and yet has failed. And why? Because he has indulged in a legal spirit—has sought salvation by the works of the law, and not by faith. This leads to another point of resemblance between the Syrian leper and the awakened sinner :—

IV. *Both are at first dissatisfied with the remedy proposed.*—Although Naaman knew that his leprosy was a loathsome and deadly disease; although he was willing to come all the way from Syria to Samaria; although he was willing to part with his talents of silver, and his pieces of gold, and his changes of raiment; although he was willing to do almost anything in the world to be cured of his leprosy, yet, when he comes to the house of the prophet, and finds how simple and humiliating are the terms proposed, his pride is wounded, and he turns away in a rage.

Mark the pride of the man! "What!" says he, "surely the prophet does not know who I am! Does he know that I am Syria's chieftain?—that I have come in pomp and splendour, with my horses and my chariot—with my silver and my gold? Does he know that I am the favourite of my king, and the idol of my countrymen?—that I am a rich man, a great man, a man of war, and a mighty man? And will he not come out and pay me that respect due to my rank and character?

"He sends a messenger to me! A messenger! I expected more than this! Behold, I thought he himself would come out to me, and stand, and call upon the Lord his God, and strike his hand over the place, and recover the leper. I thought he would cure me in a manner comporting with my dignity. But not so. He sends a messenger to me!

"And, pray, what is his message? He tells me to go and bathe in Jordan seven times! And why in Jordan? Does not that contemptible stream belong to that contemptible people, many of whom I have recently conquered, and led captive into my own land? Then, why in Jordan? I see what the man would be aiming at! He would have me dip in Jordan, and thus acknowledge myself indebted to the Jews for a cure!—I

will die a leper first! What! such a man as I!—
a rich man, a great man, a mighty man, the conqueror of the Jews—such a man as I am, acknowledge myself indebted to the Jews for a cure!
Not I! I'll die a leper a thousand times first!
' Are not Abana and Pharpar, rivers of Damascus,
better than all the waters of Israel? May I not
wash in them, and be clean?' " So he turned
and went away in a rage.

Wretched man! he would be wretched, because
he would be proud. He is a leper, a loathsome
leper, and yet he would be proud!

What an admirable picture of the natural or
unrenewed man! How exact to the very life!
The sinner is a leper; he knows that the leprosy
of sin is upon him; that it has spread over his
whole moral system; that it is working disease
and death within him, and if not removed, will
cut him off from heaven, and ruin him for ever.
In these circumstances, he asks with more or less
anxiety, what he must do to be saved; and when
told, " Believe in the Lord Jesus Christ, and be
saved "—oh, these terms are too hard and unreasonable! They are too simple—too humbling.
They do not suit his proud and lofty soul; and he
turns away in a rage.

Yes, the heart of the sinner rises up against
this way of salvation. Sometimes there is a positive enmity awakened, and the sinner would almost

rather not be saved at all, than to be saved in a manner so galling to his proud and carnal heart. If salvation were put up at auction, he would bid high for it; but to be saved in the way pointed out in the gospel—this does not suit his taste—does not fall in with the feelings of his unsanctified heart! He objects to this plan; he turns away from it, and would choose rather to be saved in some other way; and when told, that "other foundation can no man lay, than that is laid, which is Jesus Christ," he does not like it; and when it is pressed upon him, like Naaman, he turns away, and is ready to say: "Are not Abana and Pharpar, rivers of Damascus, better than all the waters of Israel? May I not wash in them and be clean?" In other words, May I not be saved in my own way?

It may here be proper to inquire why the sinner is not pleased with the plan proposed in the gospel. One might suppose that the sinner, feeling himself to be a sinner, and knowing himself to be exposed to the wrath and curse of God, would be willing to be saved in any way. But no, we find it a universal fact, that the sinner tries his own plans first, and never will fall in with Heaven's plan, until he finds that absolutely he must, or else perish for ever. The fact is well known; the reasons may be these:

First: the plan of salvation proposed in the

gospel strips the sinner of his self-righteousness. All unconverted persons, but especially those who have been more moral and genteel, those who have moved in respectable circles, and who have been classed with the benevolent and honourable ones of the day, are apt to imagine that they have something to recommend them, even in the sight of God their Maker. They are sinners, no doubt, but not great sinners.

"Why! what harm have I done? I have injured no man; I have defrauded no man; I am no liar, no drunkard, no gambler; I never swear, except when I am angry; I pay all my just debts; I have a respect for good ministers, and go to hear them, and, according to my means, I contribute to their support. Moreover, I am a member of the Bible Society, and give to many benevolent institutions; and now, pray, what lack I yet?"

The sum of the matter is this: the sinner begins with the confession that he is a sinner, and winds up with the belief that he is a pretty good man, and that his good deeds entitle him, at least, to some consideration. But the gospel comes and addresses him, not as a pretty good man, but as a sinner, a great sinner, a lost and ruined sinner. The gospel tells him that his heart is deceitful above all things, and desperately wicked; that his whole life has been a life of departure from God; that his best actions have been mixed with sin; and that, in the sight of his Maker, all his righteousnesses are as filthy rags; that the prayer of the publican suits him as truly as any other, and that if he ever is saved, it must be purely by grace, and in Christ alone.

Now this does not fall in with his self-righteous feelings. He wishes some respect shown to him, on account of his being rather better than some others; and is not willing to be placed on the same platform with the vilest of sinners, and, like them, be saved entirely on the score of free grace. This is too humbling to the pride of his heart; and when he is told that it is even so, that in the sight of God he also is a great sinner, a vile sinner, and if ever saved, " Christ must be all his hope, and grace all his song:" this doctrine does not suit him; and, when insisted upon, he is displeased, and turns away in a rage.

Unhappy sinner! He would be unhappy because he would be self-righteous and proud. Oh, how hard it is for the sinner to feel that he is a sinner, a guilty, hell-deserving sinner! How hard for him to realize that he lies low in the ruins of the fall! that in the sight of a pure and holy God he is vile, and, if ever saved, it must be by grace, and by grace alone! This is so galling, so humbling to his proud and lofty soul. Pride is in his very nature. Oh, this pride, this abominable pride! How it blocks up the way to

heaven ! How it bars up against him the gates
of glory ! Now, permit me to say, this pride
must be brought down—as it is written, "The
Lord resisteth the proud, but giveth grace unto
the humble." And again, " The loftiness of man
shall be bowed down, and the haughtiness of men
shall be laid low ; and the Lord alone shall be exalted in that day." '

Secondly : Another reason why the sinner
does not, at first, like the plan proposed in the
gospel is this — On account of the self-denial
which it exacts.

"Deny thyself and take thy cross,
Is the Redeemer's great command."

Now, this is a hard saying. Who can hear it ?
The sinner, perhaps, is young, and in the midst
of all the pleasurable scenes of life ; and he is
told, if he becomes a Christian he must deny
himself; he must renounce the world, with all
its pomps and vanities; he must come out from
the world, withdraw from places of fashionable
resort, give up all sinful pleasures ; he must break
away from his irreligious companions, no longer
go with them in the flowery and devious paths of
sin. The spirit of the world he must not indulge
in. He must repudiate its maxims, its manners,
and everything that is opposed to the genius of a

religion that is holy, and heavenly, and divine.
He must not suffer "the lust of the flesh, nor
the lust of the eye, nor the pride of life," to have
dominion over him any more. He must set his
face and heart against sin of every kind, whether
fashionable or unfashionable, whether profitable or
unprofitable, whether pleasurable or not. He must
be willing to take the yoke of Christ upon him,
and maintain a holy singularity; ay, and "touch
not, taste not, handle not" anything that is
offensive to God, or polluting to the soul.

This is not pleasant to the sinner. He is willing to give up some sins, but not all — some
worldly amusements, but not all. He does not
like strict rules; he does not like religious re-
straints. He wishes to go along with the world,
at least to a certain extent. He wishes to have
some latitude in the matter of worldly pursuits
and pleasures, and he does not like to be so bound
up as not to be permitted, occasionally, to attend
dancing parties in the evening, and pleasurable ex-
cursions on the Sabbath, or to resent injuries. He
is much disposed to compromise matters; to enjoy
religion and the world too. But the gospel is
stern and uncompromising. The sinner must
give up every sin; though dear as a right eye, he
must pluck it out; though dear as a right hand,
he must cut it off. Yea, he must live denied to *all*
ungodliness and worldly lusts, and live soberly,

and righteously, and godly, in this present world.
Now, thinks he, is not this carrying matters a
little too far? Is not this fanaticism? What is
the use of being so strict and strait-laced? What
is the use of being righteous overmuch? May
not a more genteel and accommodating religion
answer just as well, and even a little better?
" Are not Abana and Pharpar, rivers of Damascus,
better than all the waters of Israel? May I not
wash in them and be clean?" So he turns away
in a rage.

Unhappy sinner! He would be unhappy, because he does not wish to deny himself of all ungodliness and worldly lust. He does not wish
entirely to let go his hold upon the world. There
is some darling sin, some beloved lust or idol,
which he wishes still to enjoy; and religion won't
let him; hence the warfare and the battle in the
sinner's soul!

A third reason why the sinner does not, at
first, like the plan proposed in the gospel, is the
spirituality which it requires. I never knew an
unregenerate man to be spiritual. He may take
much pleasure in forms and ceremonies, but for
that which is truly spiritual he has no relish. The
homage of a lip-service, and the compliment of a
bended knee, he may be willing to offer to his
Maker, but his heart is not in the matter. His
spirit is not devout—never truly and deeply devout.

He runs over the surface of things, and greatly prefers the form to the power of godliness. He takes no pleasure in drawing near to God, nor is he much inclined to pray in secret, nor to worship God, who is a Spirit, in spirit and in truth. He has no objection, it may be, to converse about religion in general, and is willing to hear what he calls a good sermon, but he is not remarkably fond of plain, pungent, and practical preaching. If the minister has an agreeable person and a fine voice; if he is graceful in his gestures and has a brilliant imagination; if he can deal in flowers of rhetoric, or spread an intellectual treat before his hearers, he can listen to him, it may be, for one full hour.

But let the man of God wax warm; let him lay aside his beautiful things, and come down to the law and to the testimony; let him speak about the claims of the law, its extent and spirituality; let him thunder out his anathemas against the sinner; let him repeat what is written—" Cursed is every one that continueth not in all things written in the book of the law to do them;" let him press the necessity of repentance and reiterate the language of the Saviour, " Except a man be born again, he cannot see the kingdom of God " —then the sinner's attention begins to flag. He begins to be restless and uneasy; thinks the sermon too long ; and secretly resolves that he will come to hear that man no more.

" I don't like these preachers these days," said a certain man who had been listening to an awakening preacher during a season of revival: " I don't like these preachers these days, they make one feel so bad." Here the secret is revealed. Whilst the minister was dealing in beautiful things, and general things, the sinner's conscience was not disturbed ; but when the claims of the law were presented, and the sinner's guilt and danger were made to start up before his mind, his carnal security was interrupted. He began to see that he was not quite so good as he had imagined himself to be. There was a sinking at his heart, an unwelcome peradventure, that, notwithstanding all his fond and cherished hopes, his state might not be so safe after all. No, no ! he does not wish religion to have full dominion over him. It will interfere with some of his pursuits and schemes, and he is much disposed to say, " Go thy way for this time ; when I have a convenient season I will call for thee."

The sinner will, perhaps, read the Bible ; but he has no particular relish for the Psalms of David, nor Paul's Epistles. He greatly prefers the narrative and historical portions, and will speak in high terms of the Bible. "The Bible ! the Bible ! " he will say, " Why, sir, the Bible is the best book in the world ! The doctrines, how sublime ! The precepts, how perfect ! The parables, how beautiful! There is the parable of the Prodigal Son, and the parable of the Good Samaritan; why, sir, these are some of the finest specimens of moral painting ever presented to an admiring world! Sooner shall the seraph's voice lose its · melody, than these parables cease to charm!"

But now, should the person with whom he is conversing say, "It pleases me much, sir, to find that you speak so highly of the sacred volume; but, as that book lays great stress upon the doctrine of the new birth, or regeneration, will you permit me to ask you one question? Do you really think, sir, that you have experienced this spiritual change, without which no one can enter heaven?"

"I would be glad," replies he, "to know what you think about infants. Do you think all infants will be saved?"

Let the pious friend rejoin, "Sir, I believe that those who die in infancy are saved; but I was not talking about infants. I was, with all respect, inquiring about your hopes for eternity. I greatly desire your salvation; I wish you to dig deep, and lay a good foundation for eternity; will you, therefore, permit me to press the question, Do you really think that you are a converted man?"

"Can you tell me, sir," says he, "who was Melchizedek? Without father, without mother, without beginning of days or end of life! Why, who can this be?"

My brethren, I suppose you understand this matter; the case is drawn from real life. The sinner is willing to talk on the subject of religion in a certain way, but he wishes not to have anything of a spiritual nature pressed upon him; nothing that will trouble his conscience, or lead to any great searchings of heart.

The fact is, as yet, he is not a spiritual man, and therefore does not like spiritual things. He has no objection to the form of godliness, but the power of it he understands not. When, therefore, he is told that he must worship God, who is a Spirit, in spirit and in truth; that he must pray in secret; that he must remember the Sabbath day to keep it holy; that he must live by faith, and walk by faith, and that he must see to it, that his heart is right in the sight of God: in a word, when spiritual duties and exercises are insisted upon, and he is told that he must continually strive to have the spirit of him who said, "Truly, our fellowship is with the Father, and with his Son, Jesus Christ"—these things, in his estimation, are hard requirements, they are distasteful to him; they are deemed unnecessary and puritanical; and when urged, he is much inclined to be offended, and, turning away in disgust, his spirit utters the language of Naaman—"Are not

Abana and Pharpar, rivers of Damascus, better than all the waters of Israel? May I not wash in them and be clean?"

Thus the sinner is still unhappy, because opposed to the gospel plan. Oh! how he longs to be saved in his own way! but the Bible will not permit him, and hence the struggles in the sinner's bosom—the warfare and the battle in the sinner's soul.

A fourth and a last reason which I shall mention, why the sinner does not, at first, relish the plan proposed in the gospel, is this: It requires him to accept the Saviour cordially, in all his offices.

In the sacred volume, the blessed Redeemer is exhibited in a great variety of characters, but in none does He appear as He should in the eyes of the sinner. Is Jesus a *Prophet?* What occasion for such a teacher to instruct him? "The light of reason," and the sentiments of the learned, he thinks, will answer just as well. Is Jesus a *Priest?* What occasion has he for such a one to intercede and atone for him? Tears of repentance, and moral reformation, he thinks, are all-sufficient to secure his pardon. Is Jesus Christ a *King* The proud sinner wants no king to rule in and reign over him. His lips are his own—who is Lord over him? Is Jesus a *Physician?* To be sure, the sinner knows that there is a moral

leprosy upon him, but he hopes the case is not
so bad after all. Why may not "the balsam of
tears" and the "opiates of morality" effect a speedy
cure? And, as for this Fountain opened in the
house of David for sin and uncleanness, what
occasion is there for that? "Are not Abana and
Pharpar, rivers of Damascus, better than all the
waters of Israel? May I not wash in them and
be clean?" So he turns away in a rage.

How exact are the points of resemblance
between Naaman and the awakened sinner!
Surely this fragment of history was recorded,
to present with liveliness, in a figure, the case of
the awakened sinner, in every place, and in every
age! One point of resemblance more, and I
have done.

V. *Both are shut up to the remedy proposed;
it is that, or death!*—This is a most important
point of resemblance, and one which must never
be forgotten. Both are shut up to the remedy
proposed; it is that, or death! When Naaman,
not pleased with the terms stated, turned away,
observe, the prophet did not call him back; the
prophet proposed no compromise. Dip in Jordan
seven times, and thou shalt be cleansed—refuse,
and take the consequences.

Even so with the sinner. Let him, by faith,
cordially accept of the Lord Jesus Christ, and he
shall be saved!—reject Him, and the sinner must

perish! Positively, there is no other hope for
him! for nothing can be more clear and settled
than this declaration—"There is salvation in none
else:" and this, "Other foundation can no man
lay than is laid, which is Jesus Christ."

And, in substance, this solemn truth was
announced by the Saviour himself, in his last
charge to his disciples: "Go ye into all the world,
and preach the gospel to every creature; he that
believeth and is baptized shall be saved; he that
believeth not, shall be damned."

There has been no change, no compromise;
there never will be! for the way of salvation,
like the Saviour himself, is the same yesterday,
to-day, and for ever. Hence the language of the
apostle: "How shall we escape if we neglect so
great salvation?" There is no escape! The
sinner who rejects Christ, rejects the only Saviour,
the only remedy. He cannot be saved by his
own works of righteousness; he cannot be saved
by the intercession of saints, nor purgatorial
sufferings. Jesus Christ is the sinner's last and
only hope, and if the sinner will not accept of
Christ, he must perish! he must die eternally!
he must be lost for ever! Oh that the sinner
would believe this truth, this great Bible truth,
and come to Christ before it is for ever too late!

When Naaman turned away from the house
of the prophet—when he resolved to return to

Syria, and brave the consequences, rather than
submit to terms so galling to the pride of his
heart—in these circumstances, it so happened
that he had with him certain servants, who seem
to have had a great respect for their master; they
greatly desired that he might be cured; and to
them the opportunity of obtaining a cure seemed
a precious one, and the terms by no means hard
or unreasonable: " And they came near unto him,
and spake unto him, and said, My father, if the
prophet had bid thee do some great thing, wouldst
thou not have done it? How much rather, when
he saith unto thee, Wash and be clean! "

The argument was a good one; Naaman felt
its force. He saw that he was a poor leper, and
that pride was not made for him! He saw that
his case was a desperate one. He could not cure
himself;—no one in Syria could remove his
leprosy. Here was an opportunity, and one only.
Had he not better be a little humbled, than live
and die a loathsome leper? Had he not better
give up his lofty notions, and take the prophet on
his own terms? Yes, the urgency of the case
demands it; and the terms are not hard. Jordan
is not far off, and how simple, how easy, to dip as
the prophet directed! Reason has triumphed!
the servants have prevailed! the proud conqueror,
the haughty Naaman, yields! " Then went he
down, and dipped himself seven times in Jordan,

according to the saying of the man of God, and his flesh came again unto him as the flesh of a little child, and he was clean!"

Methinks I see him coming out of Jordan, cleansed of his leprosy—a new man! How his eyes sparkle! What joy beams in every feature of his countenance! He smiles! He can scarcely believe in the change wrought! It is too good to be true! Surely it must be some sweet dream! "Servants! is it true? Is your master's leprosy gone?"—"Yes, master, gone! It is just as the prophet has said. Your face is fair and beautiful; your flesh is as the flesh of a little child!"

"O blessed prophet! O faithful servants! O happy, happy me!" methinks I hear the Syrian exclaim. "Yes, blessed prophet! faithful servants! and happy! happy! thrice happy me! What a blessed hour! what a blessed change is this to me! How I rejoice that my pride came down! How glad I am that I came to the house of the prophet, and especially, that I at length yielded to his terms! This is the happiest hour of my life; more happy than when, on the field of battle, I proved a conqueror! more happy than when I was welcomed home, with greetings, and acclamations, by my royal master, and my grateful countrymen! And now, when I return to Syria, and all shall see that my leprosy is cleansed, how with new joy they will greet me again! Will not my wife be made happy? Will not all my acquaintances be filled with wonder and delight! Yes, the voice of joy and gratulation will salute me on every hand! Surely, we shall have a blessed jubilee!"

Is there an awakened sinner here? Is there one in this large assembly who is sensible that a spiritual leprosy cleaves to him? Is he distressed by reason of his disease? Is he willing to go far and do much to obtain a cure? And yet, is he dissatisfied with Heaven's plan of saving the sinner? Is he in the indulgence of a proud and self-righteous spirit, endeavouring to work out his own salvation in his own way? Is he unwilling to humble himself at the foot of the cross—unwilling to be wholly indebted to Christ for salvation?

If there be such a one present, I would act towards him as Naaman's servants did towards the Syrian leper. I would come near, I would reason, I would expostulate, I would entreat. My father! my mother! my friend! Oh my fellow-sinner! if the prophet—if Jesus Christ had bid you do some great thing, would you not have done it? How much rather, when He says, Wash and be clean! If He had bid you traverse oceans and scale mountains; if He had bid you brave the fury and storm of battle; if He had bid you bestow all your goods to feed the poor, and give your body to be burned—would you not have been willing to do all this, and even more, to secure your salvation ?   How much rather, then, when He says, " Come unto Me, all ye that are weary and heavy laden, and I will give you rest." " Look unto Me and be saved, all ye ends of the earth, for I am God, and beside Me there is none else."   Oh how simple is the way of salvation ! " Believe in the Lord Jesus Christ, and thou shalt be saved."

The sinner cannot save himself. He is not required to do it. A Saviour is provided, an all sufficient and most glorious Saviour—one who is able and willing to save unto the uttermost, all who will come unto God through Him. This blessed Saviour, having made the great atoning sacrifice, can bestow pardon and life upon the very chief of sinners, the vilest of the vile. Only let the sinner come to Christ, in all the over-flowings of a penitent and believing heart, his leprosy will be cleansed, his pardon will be sealed.

Awakened sinner ! this is the way ! How simple !   Stumble not at its simplicity. How reasonable !   Then quarrel no longer with Heaven's plan. Again I say, if the prophet— if Jesus Christ had bid you do some great thing, would you not have done it ? how much rather when He says, " Wash and be clean—believe and be saved."

What hinders you? Is it a self-righteous spirit? Are you righteous in God's account? Remember, He is a thrice holy God, and cannot look upon sin with the least allowance. Are you righteous even in your own account? Has your conscience never troubled you? Do you not know, do you not feel that you are a sinner—that your sins are numerous, and highly aggravated? How do you propose to get rid of your sins? They cleave to you; no mortal power can remove them. Believe me, in the sight of a pure and holy God you would have no righteousness to boast of, even if you were as pure a man as Isaiah; for he confessed that all his righteousnesses were as filthy rags; and, on a certain occasion, he cried out, "Woe is me, for I am undone, for I am a man of unclean lips, and I dwell in the midst of a people of unclean lips, for mine eyes have seen the King, the Lord of hosts!"

But I ask again, what hinders the sinner from falling in with the gospel plan? He is proud—too proud to be saved by free grace—too proud to be indebted to Christ alone for salvation. Proud! and proud of what? Of a rebellious will? of a seared conscience? of a sinful life? of a hard heart? Proud! Of what? That he is a loathsome leper? a condemned sinner? an heir of wrath? and a child of the devil? Proud! Of what? Of riches? Some of the vilest on earth are rich. Of beauty? Beauty! "The grave discredits thee. How are thy charms expunged! thy roses faded, and thy lilies soiled!" Proud! Of what? Of talents? "With the talents of an angel a man may be a fool." Proud! Of what? Of splendour and renown? "Behold, the Lord of hosts doth take away the mighty man, and the man of war, the judge, and the prophet, and the prudent, and the ancient, the captain of fifty, and the honourable man, and the counsellor, and the cunning artificer, and the eloquent orator."

Ah! my brethren! pride was never made for man. The sick chamber may teach him this, and so, emphatically, may death and the grave. A sinner proud! One whose soul is a mass of sin, and whose body must soon moulder in the tomb! He proud! How preposterous and absurd! I repeat it, pride was never made for poor sinful man. No! the dust is his place, and the prayer of the publican his appropriate prayer: "God be merciful to me a sinner."

And now, haughty Naaman, let your pride come down. Turn your chariot, and go to Jordan. Yield, oh yield to the terms of the prophet, and let your leprosy pass away! O sinner! sinner! be persuaded to fall in with the terms of the gospel! Yield your heart to Christ; you will never repent it. Did Naaman repent complying with the terms of the prophet? No, he rejoiced with exceeding great joy—he rejoiced in it to his dying day! And so will you, and not to your dying day only, but to all eternity.

I have seen sinners coming to Christ. I have seen them in the day of their conversion. Oh, what a blessed moment! what a glorious change! The soul has new feelings; the heart has new joy! Everything within is pleasant; everything around is lovely. The sun shines more brightly, and the birds sing more sweetly. The flowers are more beautiful, and even the grass looks more green. Yes, it is even so. Sometimes the young convert feels as if he had entered into a new world—rejoices with joy unspeakable and full of glory—yea, "has a young heaven begun below, and glory in the bud."

Tell me not that this is fanaticism! If it be, it is the fanaticism of the pentecostal converts, for we are told that "they did eat their meat with gladness and singleness of heart, praising God." It is the fanaticism of those who were converted in Samaria, for we are told that "there was great joy in that city." When the Philippian jailer was converted, according to the Scriptures he rejoiced in God with all his house. And what is said of the eunuch when he was brought under the influence of God's converting grace? "He," also, "went on his way rejoicing." This is no fanaticism. It is all perfectly reasonable and natural. Should a poor man suddenly become rich, or a sick man all at once find himself in strong health—should a person who was sleeping in a dungeon wake up in a palace, or he who was in a wilderness find himself in a garden, how sweet would be the surprise! how delightful the feelings! Even so it is with him who passes from a state of nature to a state of grace.

> " When God revealed his gracious name,
>   And changed my mournful state ;
>   My rapture seemed a pleasing dream,
>   The grace appeared so great ! "

Well may there be joy, yea "rapture," in the soul, seeing that everything in relation to the sinner has undergone so great and pleasing a change. The bond-slave of the devil has become the freedman of Christ, and the heir of wrath an heir of glory! Oh that many hearts may even now yield, and may this be the birthday of many a precious soul!

When Naaman returned to Syria cleansed of his leprosy, no doubt there were rejoicings there! How joyfully must his friends have greeted him, now returned safe and sound! and oh how happy, especially, must have been his kindred, the members of his own family! Surely the voice of joy and gratulation was heard on every hand! Surely there must have been a jubilee for many days! And now, should the awakened sinner come to

Christ, what joy would this inspire in many
bosoms! This would be an occasion long to be
remembered. Yes, only let these anxious souls
who are now weeping—only let them now come
to Christ, and we shall have a jubilee here too!
Oh, how that pious father would rejoice in the
conversion of his son! How that pious mother,
who for years has been praying for her daughter—
how she would press to her bosom with feelings
of new delight that beloved daughter, once care-
less, now a Mary at the feet of her Redeemer!
How would the pious wife rejoice over the conversion of her husband! and the pious husband
over the conversion of his wife! How brothers
and sisters would rush into each other's arms, and
give glory to God, that now, at last, they were
going to heaven hand in hand! I have beheld
such scenes. They bring us near to heaven.

Oh for the yielding of hearts! the breaking
of strongholds! God grant us a pentecostal time,
a blessed jubilee now, even in this place and at
this time! O Lord, revive thy work! Let the
people praise Thee, let all this people praise Thee!
Amen, and Amen!

ON SEEKING THE LORD.

"Seek ye the Lord while He may be found, call ye upon Him while He is near."—ISAIAH iv. 6.

MY brethren, if a man wants wealth, he seeks it; if he desires fame, he seeks it; if he has set his heart upon the attainment of any temporal object which he deems important, he makes a diligent use of the proper means for the attainment of that object. This principle is correct, and upon it is based the words of our text: "Seek ye the Lord while He may be found, call ye upon Him while He is near." David said, "When thou saidst, Seek ye my face, my heart said unto thee, Thy face, Lord, will I seek." Hezekiah was commended because he sought the Lord with all his heart; and Josiah, because he sought the Lord whilst he was young. The direction in our text is a standing one:—"Seek ye the Lord while He may be found, call ye upon Him while He is near."

Some persons are ready to say, "You ministers of the gospel are frequently urging us to attend to the great concern, and warning us of the danger of dying in our sins, but why do you not pour a little light upon the subject? Why do you not tell us plainly what we are to do?" Well, now, if I tell you what is to be done, will you attend to it? If I mark out the way to heaven, will you walk in it? Then listen! If you would be saved, you must seek the Lord, and if you would do this successfully, there are three things which must be done. You must take Jesus Christ for your way; the Divine Spirit for your helper; and the sacred volume for your guide.

To be sure, I might say to the serious inquirer, as Paul did to the Philippian jailer, " Believe on the Lord Jesus Christ, and thou shalt be saved;" or, as Peter did to certain Jerusalem sinners, when awakened, " Repent ye, therefore, and be converted, that your sins may be blotted out, when the times of refreshing shall come from the presence of the Lord." But you wish me to be more extended in my remarks, then let me call your attention to the three things stated.

I. You are to take Jesus Christ as your way; and for this we have his own authority, as He expressly says, "I am the way, the truth, and the life" (or, as it may be rendered, " the true and living way"), " and no man cometh unto the Father but by Me." In the economy of redemption Jesus Christ is "all and in all." He is our only Advocate and Mediator. "God was in Him, reconciling the world unto Himself, not imputing to them their iniquities!" but, out of Christ, God is a consuming fire. Those who are accepted, are accepted in the Beloved, and those who are not accepted in the Beloved, are not accepted at all; as it is written, "Other foundation can no man lay than is laid, which is Jesus Christ."

This is all very plain, and this in substance is taught by every true minister of Christ, on every Sabbath-day; and yet many persons, when awakened, and when stirred up to seek the salvation of their souls, make an error at the very outset. They go to God the Father without having any reference to Christ, as the appointed Mediator. Now, this will not answer, for the Saviour says expressly, in language already recited, "I am the way, the truth, and the life, and no man cometh unto the Father but by Me." There was corn in Egypt when the famine prevailed, and when those who needed corn came unto Pharaoh, he said unto them, Go to Joseph, I have made him lord over all Egypt, therefore go to Joseph. Should they neglect this direction, and come to Pharaoh the second time, methinks he would say, Did I not tell you to go to Joseph? he is appointed over this matter. Go to Joseph. Should they come to Pharaoh the third time, without regarding his

direction, methinks he would say, Leave my kingdom instantly !—no man who will not submit
to the law of the realm shall receive supplies.
Leave my kingdom without delay !—Even so
in this matter. Christ is Lord of all, and without Him there is no salvation, and there is no
hope.

But again ; some persons, setting out to seek
the salvation of their souls, make another blunder.
Instead of coming to Christ in the exercise of
love, and an appropriating faith, they go to their
duties. They think that they are not good enough
to come to Christ yet, and therefore they pur-
pose to make themselves a little better first ; just
like those of whom Paul speaks, who, " being
ignorant of God's righteousness, and going about
to establish their own righteousness, have not
submitted themselves unto the righteousness of
God" (Rom. x. 3). And why is this? Because
this great doctrine is forgotten, or not properly
understood, that " Christ is the end of the law
for righteousness to every one that believeth ;" and
as the apostle teaches in another place, that " a
man is justified by faith without the deeds of the
law " (Rom. iii. 28).

My brethren, I repeat it, in the economy of
redemption Christ is all in all. This must be
clearly understood and acted upon by all who
would seek the Lord and find Him in the salvation

of their souls. The language of the poet is both
beautiful and correct :

"Jesus ! lover of my soul,
　Let me to thy bosom fly,
While the raging billows roll,
　While the tempest still is high.
Hide me, O my Saviour, hide,
　Till the storm of life is past ;
Safe into the haven guide ;
　Oh, receive my soul at last !

" Other refuge have I none !—
　Hangs my helpless soul on Thee ;
Leave, ah! leave me not alone,
　Still support and comfort me.
All my trust on Thee is stayed,
　All my help from Thee I bring;
Cover my defenceless head
　With the shadow of thy wing."

II. You must take the Divine Spirit as your
helper. Even if the sinner were pardoned by
virtue of the redemption which is in Christ Jesus,
there is still an inward work of grace and sancti-
fication to be accomplished, to fit him for heaven.
And, as the angel of the Lord said unto Elijah,
" Arise and eat, because the journey is too great
for thee," so may we say to the awakened sinner,
who asks what he must do to be saved, " Arise and
seek divine aid, for the work is too great for thee."

For example, the sinner's heart is to be changed.
As it is written, " O Jerusalem, wash thy heart

from wickedness, that thou mayest be saved!"
(Jer. iv. 14.) And again: "Make you a new
heart, and a new spirit: for why will ye die,
O house of Israel?" (Ezek. xviii. 31.) Now, the
sinner, of himself, can no more accomplish this
great work than he can roll a mountain, or heave
an ocean! What then? Shall he say, I cannot
accomplish the work—it is the work of the Spirit:
his influences are absolutely necessary; I will
leave it to the Spirit; and I will do nothing.
Shall he say this? Certainly not. The showers
of heaven we all know are absolutely necessary to
the production of a crop. Planters! if God should
seal up the clouds of heaven, and send no rain
upon the earth for three years and six months, as
in the time of the prophet, you might fence in
your field, and plough up your ground, and scatter
your seed; but it would be all in vain. What
then? Does the planter say, "The showers of
heaven are absolutely necessary to the production
of a crop; I will do nothing—I will sit still and
leave it to the showers of heaven to fence in my
field, and plough up my ground, and scatter the
seed. Does he say this? We know that he does
not. Well, the winds of heaven, also, are necessary to waft the merchant-ship over the ocean.
The shipmaster knows it full well; and does he
say, I will not weigh the anchor—I will not
spread the canvas—I will not consult the chart—

the winds of heaven are absolutely necessary to waft my ship over the ocean—I will leave it all to the winds of heaven ? Oh no, we never hear anything of this kind.

In temporal matters sinners usually act wisely and discreetly; but in spiritual matters all seem to be perverse and wrong. There need be no difficulty. As in temporal so in spiritual matters. There must be the meeting of the divine and human agency. See the children of Israel at Pihahiroth; they are hemmed in on all sides; mountains on this side, mountains on that side; behind them, Pharaoh with his army pressing on; and before them the Red Sea ! Now, are they not completely hemmed in ? They are unarmed, and it is clear deliverance can come only from above. But they were delivered. How ? By the meeting of the human and divine agency :—God directs Moses to stretch his rod over the Red Sea. Moses, if perverse, might have said, Lord God, what is the use of stretching the rod over the Red Sea ? He was not perverse. The command was given : Stretch the rod over the Red Sea. He obeyed — he stretched the rod. Here was the putting forth of the human agency. Immediately the divine agency came down with mighty power upon the waters of the Red Sea, and lo ! they parted asunder, and the children of Israel passed through on dry ground ! Now, here was the meeting of both the divine and human agency, and yet all who looked on knew very well that the only efficient agent was God; hence the tribes, with one accord, on the other side of the banks of the Red Sea, sang God's praises, not the praises of Moses.

Take another case. The children of Israel, in the wilderness, on a certain occasion, were ready. to perish with thirst—

> "They longed for a cooling stream,
> And they must drink or die."

And now, who can furnish water for such a multitude in this parched waste and howling wilderness? Assuredly, none but God only. It was furnished—how? and in what manner? By the meeting of the human and divine agency, as we said before. God directs Moses to reach forth his rod and smite the rock. He did so, and lo! the water gushed in great abundance from the smitten rock. The children of Israel crowded around, drank of the cool flowing stream, slaked their thirst, and praised, not Moses, but the God of Israel; for all saw plainly, that, although Moses smote the rock, it was God, and God only, who caused the water to gush forth.

I repeat it, my brethren, there need be no difficulty in understanding this matter. The work to be accomplished is great, utterly beyond the sinner's power; but he may obtain help from on high. As it is written, "Let him take hold of my strength, that he may make peace with Me, and he shall make peace with Me" (Isa. xxvii. 5). And again: "Fear not, I am with thee, I will help thee, I will strengthen thee, yea I will uphold thee with the right hand of my righteousness." I am aware that this last passage has special reference to the people of God who are in trouble, but certainly it may be quoted for the encouragement of all who, sensible that they need help from above, are disposed to call upon God in sincerity and in truth; for the command given to all is this: "Seek the Lord, and his strength; seek his face evermore" (Psa. cv. 4).

Some persons, speaking on the subject of man's ability and inability, have indulged in metaphysical speculations, and have brought a vast amount of learned lore to bear upon the subject, and after all, have only darkened counsel by words without knowledge; and I have frequently thought that their account of the matter is no better than Doctor Johnson's definition of the term network: "Anything reticulated or decussated, with interstices at equal distances between the intersections." This is a very learned definition of a very simple thing; but, although learned and rather hard to be understood, it is after all, I believe, not correct; for, to constitute "network," it is not necessary that the reticulations should be at equal distances between the intersections.

But to return to the doctrine of man's ability and inability, permit me to say, there is one passage of Scripture which is worth whole volumes of merely human composition. It is this: "Work out your own salvation with fear and trembling: for it is God which worketh in you both to will and to do of his good pleasure" (Phil. ii. 12). The idea is this: that we are to attend to our soul's salvation as if we could by our own unaided effort accomplish the object in view, and at the same time rely upon divine aid, as if we literally could do nothing at all. God is ever ready to help those who are disposed to bestir themselves, and look to Him for help. Let the cry of the sinner then be the cry of the Syrophœnician woman, "Lord help me!" or the cry of Peter sinking in the water, "Lord, save, or I perish!" All this falls in precisely with the language of our text: "Seek ye the Lord while He may be found; call ye upon Him while He is near." Once more:

III. You must take the sacred volume for your guide.—It will not do to follow our own fancies, nor square our conduct by the rules which men may prescribe. No, we must, with the simplicity of little children, find out the directions which are laid down in the Scriptures of truth, and follow them. Now, in the sacred volume certain things are laid down as important, indeed as indispensable, and these must not be neglected. If you would seek the Lord and find Him the salvation of your souls,

1. You must seek Him in the forsaking of all your sins. This is a direction which immediately follows the words of our text—" Let the wicked forsake his way, and the unrighteous man his thoughts : let him return unto the Lord, and He will have mercy upon him, and to our God, for He will abundantly pardon." Yes, if the sinner would be saved, he must part with every sin. Though dear as a right hand, he must cut it off ; though dear as a right eye, he must pluck it out. Some persons, when awakened, are willing to part with some sins, but not others. There is some darling idol, some beloved lust, or what the apostle calls " besetting sin," which they are not willing to give up ; but they must give it up, for Christ came not to be the minister of sin, but to cleanse us from all unrighteousness. " His name shall be called Jesus," said the angel, " for He shall save his people from their sins." Mark ! shall save his people, not *in* their sins, but *from* their sins ; and this may remind us of the words of the Psalmist, uttered so many ages since—" If I regard iniquity in my heart, the Lord will not

hear me." Observe—not merely, if he indulges sin in his life, but sin in his heart.

I repeat it, then, there can be no compromise in this matter. Sin must be relinquished, every sin; yea, *every* sin, whether open or secret; whether fashionable or unfashionable; whether gainful or the reverse; whether it be in the life or only in the heart. Some may think this a hard requirement, but it is right, and it must stand. Some persons, as we have said, are willing to part with many sins, but not with all, and this holds them in check. They think that they are in peculiar circumstances, and desire some little indulgence in certain matters. Concerning this and that favourite sin they are ready to say with Lot, in reference to Zoar, "Oh, is it not a little one?" or with Naaman, in relation to a certain matter, "The Lord pardon thy servant in this thing." Oh these favourite, these besetting sins, how hard is it to give them up!

I recollect a certain man—pride was his besetting sin. He seemed to be constitutionally proud and haughty. He was under serious impressions a long time, and it was only when he was laid upon a bed of sickness, and brought to the borders of the grave, that his pride was subdued. I recollect another who was intemperate. He was a tavern-keeper. Powerfully wrought upon, he attended an inquiry meeting. As I

approached to the seat which he occupied, he rose
up, and with much emotion took me by the hand.
(I give you the substance of our conversation.)
"Oh, sir," said he, "I feel that I am a sinner;
what must I do to be saved?" "Sir," replied I,
"you must give up your bottle." A little nettled,
he replied, "I do not choose to make rash promises." "Very well," said I, "you may do as
you please, but I tell you the truth; you must
give up your bottle or your soul." He mused
awhile, and finally concluding, it seems, that his
bottle was worth more than his soul, he gathered
up his hat and cane and walked out, and I saw
him no more. Like Esau, my dear friends, like
Esau, "who for one morsel of meat sold his
birthright; and ye know how that afterwards,
when he would have inherited the blessing, he
was rejected, for he found no place of repentance,
though he sought it carefully with tears." Oh
these besetting sins, they have ruined many!

Another case may be mentioned. A certain
individual was brought under very pungent conviction. He cried for mercy, but for several days
received no comfort. He had had a difficulty with
a certain person some time before, and upon
examining his heart, he found that he indulged in
an unforgiving spirit. Certainly, it is all plain
now. The Saviour says, "If ye forgive not men
their trespasses, neither will your Father which is

in heaven forgive you your trespasses." This man owed his Maker ten thousand talents, and was crying for forgiveness, and yet he himself would not forgive a fellow-creature who owed him fifty pence!

Ah! my brethren, we are taught to pray—"Forgive us our trespasses as we forgive those who trespass against us." When, therefore, we utter this petition, and do not forgive those who have injured us, we do virtually pray that God will not forgive us. Remember, God knows what is within us as well as what is without us, and the Psalmist says, "If I regard iniquity in my heart, the Lord will not hear me."

Let me mention yet another case illustrative of the point before us :—In a certain town in Virginia there was a revival of religion. Amongst the anxious who came to the meeting as inquirers on a certain day, was a talented young lawyer. He appeared to be in very great distress of mind. "O sir," exclaimed he, in agony, "must I be everlastingly damned!" "By no means," said I, "my dear sir, by no means. It is a faithful saying, and worthy of all acceptation, that Christ Jesus came into the world to save sinners, even the chief. Believe in the Lord Jesus Christ and thou shalt be saved." He left the meeting still unrelieved. What can be the matter?

The case was this :—He had just commenced

the practice of the law. It was, with him, a favourite pursuit, and from this quarter he expected wealth and distinction. When brought under conviction, he recollected a prediction uttered by an aunt of his upon her dying bed, some time before, that he would yet be converted, and become a preacher of the gospel. Now, thought he, my aunt's prediction is coming true; I am going now to be converted, and then I shall have to give up my profession as a lawyer and become a preacher. This he could not consent to—would almost rather be damned than become a preacher.

Now, my brethren, observe, I do not say it is wrong for a young man to be a lawyer, but it is very wrong, very sinful, to be self-willed. This was the difficulty with this young man. He wished to have his own way; he did not wish any one, not even the ever blessed God, to cross his path; and it was whilst in this frame of mind he exclaimed, "And must I be everlastingly damned?" A few days afterwards, his will being sweetly subdued, he obtained a joyful hope in Christ, and being asked, "Mr. B——, are you willing to be a preacher now, if God shall so direct?" clasping his hands, and looking with eyes streaming with tears, he said, "Anything now! Blessed God, anything now!"

My dear friends, you that are now under

awakening influences, let me entreat you to look into your hearts, as well as your lives, and when you are told that you must seek the Lord in the forsaking of all your sins, oh remember, I pray you, in connection with it, the words of the Psalmist, already more than once repeated—" If I regard iniquity in my heart, the Lord will not hear me."

2. You must seek Him at the right time. " Seek ye the Lord while He may be found, call ye upon Him while He is near." Those guilty spirits upon whom the light of eternity has dawned, cannot seek Him now, for their day of grace is past. By them God cannot now be found; to them He is not near, nor ever will be. Their glass is run, their sun is set, and their souls are lost for ever ! The living ! the living ! those who are on mercy's side of eternity—they are the ones who may seek the Lord; and they are to do it whilst yet they are in the land of hope, and whilst yet permitted to enjoy the means of grace, and entertain the hope of glory. But, as there is such a thing as seed time, and harvest time, so there are certain seasons more favourable than others for attending to the great concern, and seeking the salvation of the soul. For example : The period of youth is a golden season; it may emphatically be called an accepted time, and day of salvation, for as yet the heart is not hardened, nor the person hackneyed in the ways of sin.

Moreover, there are special promises addressed to the young: " I love them that love Me, and they that seek Me early shall find Me;" and to them a special command is given, " Remember now thy Creator in the days of thy youth, while the evil days come not, nor the years draw nigh when thou shalt say, I have no pleasure in them." Hence we find that an overwhelming majority of those who are pious are brought in, in the morning of life. Indeed, comparatively speaking, there are few soundly converted after thirty years of age. If any one passes the period of youth, a stranger to regeneration, I consider that his best day is over, and that his prospect for heaven is darkening horribly! Oh, my dear young friends, precious youth, you are the hope of the church! Upon you many eyes are turned, and for you many prayers are offered—remember, this is emphatically your time, and it may be with you, now or never!

A season of revival is also a peculiarly favourable season for seeking the salvation of the soul. Besides divine influences coming down as copious dews and showers of rain upon a thirsty land, softening and mellowing the soil, there are special advantages, and special means of grace enjoyed. Religious meetings are multiplied, sermons more pungent, prayers more fervent, spiritual conversation more frequent; and then there is the rousing intelligence that this friend is awakened, and that converted; and who does not know that young converts are, usually, not inactive. Having found the one pearl of great price, they greatly desire to see their old companions in the possession of the same blessing. Having experienced the grace of God in their own hearts, they cannot but "tell to those around, what a dear Saviour they have found." With David they are inclined to say to every unconverted friend, " Oh, taste, and see that the Lord is good;" and as Moses said to Hobab, his brother-in-law, so are they ready to say to every dear relative, "We are journeying unto the place of which the Lord said, I will give it you: come thou with us, and we will do thee good: for the Lord hath spoken good concerning Israel." Here are new means of grace enjoyed, new appeals made, new considerations presented. In short, all the scenes and circumstances of the case are eminently calculated to awaken serious thought in the bosom, and rouse the soul to an immediate consideration of the high claims of God and eternity.

Surely then a season of revival is a precious season—it is a golden opportunity afforded for attending to the interests of the undying soul. Do not, I beseech you, do not let such a season pass unimproved. The time may come when you may desire to see the things which you now see, and shall not see them ; and to hear the things which you now hear, and shall not hear them. Yes, the time may come when you shall have to take up the dismal lamentation, " I have lost my day; the harvest is past, the summer is ended, and I am not saved."

Again : when the Spirit is striving is another peculiarly favourable season for seeking the salvation of the soul. We may not be able to explain or understand how the Divine Spirit operates upon the mind of man, but that there is such an operation there can be no doubt, for the Scriptures affirm it, and that these operations are more powerful at one time than another cannot be denied ; for sometimes the word of God is made to burn upon the conscience in a very peculiar manner, and a new concern in relation to spiritual things, is waked up in the soul. There is a more realizing sense of the vanity of the world, of the importance of religion, than common ; moreover, the person has a livelier sense of his own sinfulness and need of a Saviour, than perhaps he ever had before. He begins to envy the lot of the pious and wishes that he too were a Christian. Now, also, he takes more interest in attending upon the ordinances of God's house, and feels more inclined to read the Scriptures than usual. This is a blessed season. Now the words of the Saviour are peculiarly applicable, " Behold, I stand at the door and knock ; if any man hear my voice and open to Me, I will come in and sup with him, and he with Me." And now this passage of Scripture, too, is peculiarly appropriate, " To-day, if ye will hear his voice, harden not your heart;" and this, " Quench not the Spirit."

· This, as we have said, is truly a blessed season, but it is moreover a critical time, for sins committed in these circumstances, are sins committed against more light and more love than ordinary, and therefore are peculiarly sinful. Oh, are there any in this large and solemn assembly under the strivings of the Spirit? Remember you are·now in peculiarly solemn circumstances. You have now come to the place where two seas meet. You may now, so to speak, be casting the die for eternity! At any rate, God is come down, by his Spirit, to talk with you; yea, you have now a loud call from heaven—beware how you turn a deaf ear to it, for it may be your last!

> "Spurn not the call to life and light,
> Regard in time the warning kind;
> That call thou may'st not always slight,
> And yet the gate of mercy find.
>
> " God's Spirit will not always strive
> With hardened, self-destroying man :
> Ye who persist his love to grieve,
> May never hear his voice again."

With great emphasis, then, may the language

of our text be sounded in your ears; and may it go thundering through all the chambers of your souls, " Seek ye the Lord while He may be found, call ye upon Him while He is near." Once more,

3. You must seek the Lord with all your heart. " Blessed are they that seek Him with the whole heart," says the Psalmist; and says the Eternal God Himself, " And ye shall seek Me, and find Me, when ye shall search for Me with all your heart" (Jer. xxix. 13.) The object in view is a great object, and demands the whole soul. Some persons seek the Lord, but they do it with a divided heart. Antagonistical principles seem to be at work within them, and they are drawn in different directions. Sometimes they are greatly excited; almost persuaded to be Christians, but something seems to hold them. They are very much like a balloon ready to ascend, but bound down to the earth by a cord; or like a tree, undermined by the torrent, and thrown upon the bosom of the stream, a current is bearing strongly upon it to sweep it along, and yet it is not swept along. And why? There are some roots binding it to the bank. Cut the roots and then it will go; but so long as the roots remain uncut, so long does it there remain, see-sawing, notwithstanding the current which bears so strongly upon it. Just so, many a sinner undermined by the power of divine truth, is thrown prostrate in deep distress and

humiliation; a current of divine influences is bearing strongly upon him, to waft him to Christ and to glory, but there are some roots binding him to the earth.

Now, the sinner must cut the roots. He must break away from all the influences of the world. He must give up everything which interferes with his duty to his Maker. He must do it or he cannot expect divine acceptance—he must do it, or he must lose his soul. For no man can serve two masters, and it is quite impossible to be earthly-minded and heavenly-minded at the same time.

I recollect making a remark of this kind from the desk, at a certain place in Virginia. On coming down from the pulpit, a gentleman came up to me—he was a lawyer of high respectability— he came up to me, and grasping my hand with emotion, said, " Stranger, you have described my case exactly. Those roots, sir, those roots—they have almost ruined me. God helping me, I'll cut the roots! " I saw decision marked in his countenance. His mind was made up to have salvation, cost what it might. No wonder that about two days after he was rejoicing in Christ, and subsequently became a much valued elder of the Church.

Ah, my brethren, it is a great matter to have the mind made up; and I have observed that when the mind is fully made up the battle is half won. Only let a person be in right down good earnest in seeking the salvation of his soul; and the blessing is nigh, even at the door. And is it not reasonable, when such great interests are at stake, that the mind should be made up? Is it not reasonable, when nothing less than eternal life is the prize, that the sinner should be in good earnest? See how it is with the man in the pursuit of wealth; he leaves no stone unturned to increase his golden store. And see the man of ambition, who pants after fame, and greatly desires to reach some post of honour and distinction; how constantly is he thinking upon the subject; how diligent is he in the use of all means for the attainment of the object in view! and if he succeed not, verily his want of success is not to be ascribed either to a want of resolution or lack of effort. And when life, temporal life, is at stake, oh what struggles, what determination then! For example: roused from his slumbers at a midnight hour, a man finds his house on fire; his determination is to make his escape. Springing from his bed without delay, he rushes to the door. Does he find that locked, he hurries to the window. Is that fastened, he cries for help, again rushes to the door, again to the window. No difficulties cause him to give over his efforts to escape; they only rouse him to still greater and more determined efforts. He loses no time, puts forth all his strength, strains every nerve to break open the window, to break down the door, and if he perishes, it is whilst struggling with all his might—if he is consumed, it is because his most vigorous and determined efforts have all proved unavailing.

Oh, if sinners would but be in such good earnest in seeking the salvation of their souls, how certainly would they attain everlasting life, how certainly would a crown of glory rest upon their heads. But, alas! when roused to make some efforts, how frequently is it the case that these efforts are not as resolute and determined as they should be. They are interrupted by this thing and that. There are difficulties in the way, and various excuses are made, at the very time that the sinner should be crying for mercy and seeking help from on high.

Nehemiah and his associates had great difficulty in building up the walls of Jerusalem, which had been broken down. They wrought with one hand, while they held a weapon in the other, and the result was this—by the good hand of God over them they succeeded; as it is written, " So built we the wall, and all the wall was joined together unto the half thereof, for the people had a mind to work." Notice the phrase, " the people had a mind to work." Here was the secret of their success—their heart was in the matter; they were in good earnest in the work in which they were engaged.

Oh, could we see this spirit of fixed and settled determination carried into religious matters; could we hear this one and that one saying with the Psalmist, " My heart is fixed, O God, my heart is fixed;" or with Joshua, " Choose you this day whom ye will serve; but as for me and my house, we will serve the Lord." Could this spirit but animate every bosom in this assembly, oh what delightful scenes would here be presented; verily, the voice of joy and gratulation would be heard in every dwelling—we should truly have a pentecostal time—yea, the millennium in miniature; for remember the promise is, " Ye shall seek Me, and find Me, when you search for Me with all your heart." Oh ye who wish a blessing from on high, lay hold upon this blessed promise, take God at his word, and eternal life is sure.

Eternal life! Oh think what a boon, what a prize this is! Eternal life! what is it? Were I a glorified spirit, I would know it; were I an adoring seraph, I would feel it; but were I a glorified spirit or an adoring seraph, I could never, no never, describe it. It is to be rescued from the ruins of the fall, and restored to the favour of God! It is to be delivered from the perils and pangs of everlasting damnation, and to be placed in possession of all the bliss and glories of an eternal world of glory! In short, it is to be saved from sin and all its consequences, and to be made unspeakably happy, and that for ever and for evermore!

A certain ship, as we are informed, was caught up by a tremendous tempest and dashed upon the rocks. The passengers and crew were precipitated into the deep; twelve persons succeeded in getting into the life-boat; one poor creature more, struggling in the water, swam up to the boat, laid his right hand upon it, and attempted to get in: but one within with a sword cut off his hand! (It was apprehended that if another was taken in the boat would sink.) But what was the poor man to do? There was no safety in the wreck; he could not swim to land, it was far out of sight —the boat! the boat! he must get into the boat, or he must perish. Struggling desperately with the rolling billows, he came up to the boat a second time, and grasped it with his left hand. That, too, was cut off! Oh, poor creature, both hands bleeding, and death looking him in the face, what must he do? "Skin for skin, all that a man hath will he give for his life." He fixed his eyes again upon the boat, he came up to it the third time, and grasped the rudder with his teeth. Pity touched the heart of those within, and rather than to cut off his head, they resolved to run the risk of all perishing together.   They took him in, and his life was saved!

Oh, sinner, you are shipwrecked—you are perishing!   There is no safety for you in the wreck, and you cannot swim to land; it is far away—do you ask what is to be done?   There is a life-boat at hand; Christ is this life-boat;— struggle, oh struggle up to Him; He will not cut off the hand which you imploringly reach out to Him!   Oh no! no!   "His heart is made of tenderness—his bowels melt with love."   Cut off your hand!   He Himself reaches out both of his arms to receive you!   Oh how ready is He to save you from perishing—how able and willing to save your soul!   Oh that this day may be with you the day of decision, the birthday of your precious souls!   Come, dear friends, everything seems now propitious!   Oh come this day, and cast in your lot with the people of God, and let us all have one lot, one Jesus, one heaven, one home!

DAVID'S CHARGE TO SOLOMON.

"And thou, Solomon my son, know thou the God of thy father, and serve Him with a perfect heart and with a willing mind : for the Lord searcheth all hearts, and understandeth all the imaginations of the thoughts : if thou seek Him, He will be found of thee ; but if thou forsake Him, He will cast thee off for ever."—I CHRON. xxviii. 9.

THESE words form a part of David's farewell address, or dying charge, to Solomon, his son, and heir of his throne.   Notwithstanding his many and acknowledged faults, David was, upon the whole, both a great and a good man.   He was a great man, for he had risen from obscurity to distinction; from being a shepherd boy to be a king, and a powerful one.   But he was also a good man.   Not to mention other things, the Book of Psalms, chiefly penned by him, is a memorial to his praise; a monument more beautiful than marble, more enduring than brass.   And what, my young friends, I wish you not to forget is this, that he devoted the morning of his days, as well as all his subsequent life, to the service of his Maker.   Yes, piety adorned his youth ; it flourished in manhood; and was to him a crown of glory in his old age.   And now, having reigned over Jerusalem forty years, and knowing that the time of his departure was near at hand, like Jacob, the venerable patriarch, and Moses, the saint of God, and Joshua, the son of Nun, he devotes the last closing scene of his life to the cause of piety and of God; and in his case, emphatically, most lovely was the closing scene, lovelier far than the sunset scene at the close of the most placid day. See the mild, bright sun sinking in the west, painting with rosy colours the fleecy clouds which, here and there, are seen reposing upon the bosom of the clear blue sky.   It is a beauteous, a lovely sight, and one upon which the eye loves to linger; but the last, closing scene in the history of a good man, when his sun of life is sinking in mild splendour to rise in more effulgent glory in another and a better world, has a beauty and a loveliness peculiarly its own.   One has said,

"The chamber where the good man meets his fate
Is privileged, beyond the common walks of virtuous life,
Quite on the verge of heaven!"

Does he speak?   Every eye is fixed; every ear is attentive; all around are anxious to catch the last words which fall from his quivering lips; they are received as the counsels of wisdom and experience—almost as the voice of an oracle or angel of God.   But the case before us is invested with peculiar interest, for it is not only a good man that is about to leave the world, but it is a great man, a mighty man, a warrior, a conqueror, and a king. This is he, who, even when a youth, was more lauded than Saul, what time returning as the vanquisher of Goliath, he was met by those who, with the timbrel and the dance, uttered his praises, saying, " Saul hath slain his thousands, and David his tens of thousands ! "

Yes, it is the far-renowned David, the king of Israel, that is about to sink into the cold embrace of death. After the example of other Old Testament worthies who had gone before him, he gives his farewell address, he gives his dying charge. Picture to yourself the scene; the chief men of Jerusalem, and the mighty men, and the princes of the blood, are assembled in the palace of the dying monarch. There, on his royal couch, is the venerable man, with his cheeks furrowed and his locks silvery with age ! and there stands that young man, Solomon, his son, in youthful bloom— Solomon, the heir of David's throne.

What silence reigns ! And now the king speaks; first he addresses the nobles of his court, giving them political counsel; and then he turns his eyes upon Solomon, and upon him now every eye is fixed. Solomon, with profound veneration, waits to hear his father's charge. It falls upon his ear: " And thou, Solomon my son, know thou

the God of thy father, and serve Him with a perfect heart and with a willing mind, for the Lord
searcheth all hearts, and understandeth all the
imaginations of the thoughts; if thou seek Him,
He will be found of thee; but if thou forsake Him,
He will cast thee off for ever!"

How unexpected is this language! How
widely different from what the nobles around,
and, no doubt, from what Solomon himself antici-
pated. Certainly he will make a charge such as
might be looked for from the mouth of a dying
warrior and a king. No doubt he will speak after
this fashion:—" Solomon, your father rose from
obscurity to distinction—from being a shepherd
boy to be a king. Your father has fought many
battles, achieved many victories; Solomon, you
are to succeed your father upon the throne;
cherish a martial spirit, push forward your victories, enlarge your dominions, twine laurels
around your brow, and thus add new splendours
to David's throne." No! not a word of this
kind is uttered. What does he say? Let us hear
it again: "And thou, Solomon, my son, know
thou the God of thy father, and serve Him with a
perfect heart, and with a willing mind: for the
Lord searcheth all hearts, and understandeth all
the imaginations of the thoughts: if thou seek
Him, He will be found of thee; but if thou forsake Him, He will cast thee off for ever."

Ah! my young friends—ye young men whose hearts are set upon the world, and the things of the world; ye who are pressing after the riches of the world, and the honours of the world, and the pleasures of the world, here you may see how these things appear in a dying hour, how they are viewed even by a dying warrior and a king. Riches are nothing—honour, fame, all worldly splendour, all worldly glory, nothing. Religion looms up then. The favour of God, that is everything; all else fades away like twinkling stars before the rising sun. And how was this great truth confirmed by Solomon himself too, when the hour of his departure grew near? You recollect his language, "Vanity of vanities, all is vanity." And again: "Let us hear," says he, "the conclusion of the whole matter: fear God and keep his commandments, for this is the whole duty of man; for God shall bring every work into judgment, with every secret thing, whether it be good or whether it be evil." Believe me, young men, the time is coming when these views will be our views. God grant we may all be prepared for that hour!

There are duties and considerations presented in our text, which claim the attention of all, but particularly of young men.

I. DUTIES.—They are expressed in these words: "My son, know thou the God of thy father, and serve Him with a perfect heart and with a willing mind." First, "Know thou the God of thy father." Taking it for granted that your parents are pious, see to it that you walk in their footsteps. The counsel of Eliphaz is good counsel : "Acquaint now thyself with God, and be at peace; thereby good shall come unto thee."

Some of you, doubtless, covet knowledge of some kind or other; some of you wish to know how you can get riches; how you can secure fame; how you can multiply friends; how you can enjoy and prolong life. Believe me, there is a kind of knowledge better than all this. "My son, know thou the God of thy father." And why should you seek to know Him? Because He is the only living and true God. He is your Creator, the source of your being; He is your Preserver; his hand is underneath and around you; it is in Him that you live, and move, and have your being. He is your Benefactor; to Him you are indebted for every comfort, every enjoyment, every breath; and He is your final Judge— you and God must meet, and it would be well for you to know who He is, and what He is, before you are called into his presence. You should know Him, not as your fancy portrays Him, but as the Bible reveals Him; as a God, not only good, but just; not only merciful, but holy; a God, not only long-suffering, but who will by no means clear the guilty; in short, you are to know Him in all the beauty, and harmony, and perfection of his whole character. Oh, think how great and glorious a being He is! and how happy are those who have Him for their friend and protector! How happy are those who, in the exercise of the spirit of adoption, can address Him in this beautiful language: "Abba, Father"! and who, after contemplating his power and grandeur, can say, with holy joy and exultation, "This God is our God, for ever and ever, He will be our guide, even unto death!"

But, you are not only to know God; you are, secondly, to serve Him. What avails knowledge, if it does not prompt to obedience? You respect your father's friend, why not serve your father's God? Do you ask what you are to do? You are in the first place to give Him your heart. This is expressly commanded, as it is written in the book of Proverbs, "My son, give Me thine heart;" and this is implied in this language of our text, "Serve Him with a perfect heart, and with a willing mind." Yes, your heart must be yielded up; "you must love the Lord your God with all your heart;" you must love Him more than you love father, or mother, or brother, or sister; more than you love your property, or your sins, or your life. Ah! this is the main thing required—the heart; the seat of the affections; let this be right, and all

will be right; for love is an all-controlling principle.

> " 'Tis love which makes our willing feet
> In swift obedience move ;
> The devils know and tremble too ;
> But Satan cannot love."

But just here, I wish to remind you of certain
things which must not be forgotten.   First : You
must serve some master or other.   " What," says
the apostle, " know ye not that to whom ye yield
ourselves servants to obey, his servants ye are
whom ye obey ?"   And what says our Saviour ?
" He that committeth sin is the servant of sin."
My second remark is this : " You cannot serve
two masters."   This is what our Saviour also
expressly affirms : " No man," says he, " can
serve two masters."   And again : " Ye cannot
serve God and Mammon."

These things being so, let it be remembered
that the two masters who claim your service are
God and the *world*, and you must have one or the
other; and, using the language of Joshua, I would
say, " Choose you this day whom ye will serve."
Now, if this choice were left to your pious mother,
or to your pious sister, or to the dying Christian,
or to the heavenly ones in glory, the choice would
soon be made, and I am sure it would be a wise
choice, and one which you would never regret.
But no one is permitted to choose for you ; each

of you must make your own choice; and I would advise you to act discreetly in this matter, for the choice which you now make may be ratified in heaven, and settled upon you for ever.

Have you a regard for the matter of justice? I hope you have. Then, sit in judgment upon the claims of these two masters; whose claims are the best, those of God or of the world? You know very well that the claims of your Maker are the best, infinitely the best. Then choose accordingly. And have you a regard for your own happiness? Then sit in judgment upon the character of these two masters—which is the best master? One is good, the other is bad. One is the very kindest of all masters. He will require nothing of you but what is perfectly reasonable; nothing but what is directly calculated to promote your best interests, and your true happiness; moreover, He will be kind to you in the hour of affliction, and will not forsake you in the hour of death: nay, more, He will finally take you to heaven, and make you happy there, unspeakably happy, and happy for ever.

With regard to the other master, the world, or the devil, is he a kind master? This master is of all others the worst. He is a cruel master, a tyrant! His requirements are oftentimes most unreasonable, and he cares not for the interest nor the happiness of his servants; not unfrequently he will require what is opposed to principle and conscience. I will give an example. Alexander Hamilton was challenged by Aaron Burr to fight a duel. This method of settling disputes was not in accordance with the feelings or judgment of General Hamilton; nay, it was in direct opposition to his principles and conscience. He left this upon record. I have read what may be termed his written protest. The amount of what he wrote was this: that he did not approve of duelling; that it was abhorrent to all his feelings; that it was against his principles and conscience; but, he added, " the world expects it, the world demands it, and therefore I must accept the challenge." And he did accept it, and did fight; and, sad to say, he fell! was suddenly snatched from his family, and laid in an untimely grave!

And now, listen to the colloquy between the master and the servant in such a case. " Fight the duel," says this stern master. " It is against my conscience," replies the servant. " Who cares for your conscience? Fight the duel!" " Well, but, my master, I have a lovely wife; she is the jewel of my heart; and if I should fall in single combat she could not survive it; she would go down broken-hearted to the grave." " And what of that? Let your wife go down broken-hearted to the grave! Who cares for your wife? Fight the duel, I command you!" " But, my master, I have a number of dear children; they are young and tender, and as yet unprovided for; and if I should at this time be cut off, they may be thrown upon the cold charities of an unfeeling world; they may even become paupers; and how can I bear to think of the evil that must come upon them?" "Who cares for your children? what if they become paupers, and even vagabonds—who cares for that? Fight the duel, I again command you!" "But, oh, my hard master, listen to me. My mother taught me, that after death comes the judgment. I am not prepared to die, and if I should be slain in this combat, I fear that my poor soul may be lost, may be damned to all eternity." "And, pray, who cares for your soul? who cares if your soul should be lost and damned to all eternity? I care not; that is a very small matter. Fight the duel, I command you!—fight the duel!"

Oh, what a cruel master this is! What a tyrant! He has no regard for your principles, or feelings, or conscience; no, nor even for the salvation of your soul. And is this the master of your choice? Are you willing to wear his iron yoke? Well, when you are crushed and ruined, whom will you have to blame but yourself? Oh, how you will reproach yourself! How you will charge yourself with madness and folly, in reject-ing the kindest of all masters, and preferring one who is a hard, unfeeling, and cruel tyrant ! Remember, if you make a bad choice, you yourself, must suffer for it : and I would now say to you, as Paul did to the Philippian jailer, who drew his sword and would have killed himself, " Do thyself no harm."

" My son, know thou the God of thy father, and serve Him." Take his yoke upon you, it is not galling, it is easy ; take his burden upon you, it is not heavy, it is light. Yes, his service is a reasonable service, it is perfect freedom, This choice, you will never repent. Believe me, the ways of wisdom are ways of pleasantness, and all her paths are peace. Believe me, or rather believe Him who cannot lie—" Godliness is profitable unto all things, having promise of the life that now is, and of that which is to come." Have you made this choice in your own heart ? Then in the next place make an open avowal, a public profession of it; yes, come out from the world, take your stand openly upon the Lord's side. Let your conduct speak this language,

> " I'm not ashamed to own my Lord,
> Nor to defend his cause."

Have moral courage. Be willing that the whole world shall know that you are a Christian, that you are a disciple of the Lord Jesus ; and that, God helping you, you are determined to

serve Him faithfully till you die. Consecrate to
his service your time, your talents, your property,
your influence, your all. Let your language be
the language of the converted soul, " Lord, what
wilt Thou have me to do ? " And if any of you
be called to serve Him in the ministry of the
word, yield promptly ;. yield cheerfully, and say
with Isaiah, " Here am I, Lord, send me." But,
if not called to preach the gospel, be sure, that in
whatever station you may be placed, the full
weight of your influence shall be on the side of
religion and morality.

And here permit me to say a few things on
the subject of temperance. In the present state
of things it is called for. Young men, with your
own eyes you have seen the evils of intemperance.
Perhaps some of your own acquaintances, perhaps some of your own companions, have fallen
victims to this vice. Oh, who can tell how great
an evil it is ! Who can tell what mischief it has
done ! We have heard of wars, which have laid
cities in ashes, and kingdoms in ruins. We have
heard of tornadoes, which have carried the plough-
share of destruction over the fairest portions of
the earth. We have heard of volcanic irruptions
rolling a tide of burning lava far and wide. We
have heard of mighty earthquakes, which in one
disastrous hour have swallowed up thousands
and tens of thousands in one wide, yawning

terrific grave!—I have heard of many such things; but here is one, perhaps more ruinous to man and his best interests than all such put together. For, whereas other evils chiefly affect the body, this reaches the soul; and whereas other evils are confined to times and places, this sweeps over the whole world, as some sirocco of the desert, or some blast from the pit! Like Death upon the pale horse, it sends a thrill of horror wherever it goes. It curses men, and curses women. It curses the body, and curses the soul. It withers everything that is beautiful, and blasts everything that is good. Poverty, and disease, and strife, and violence, and murder, are in its train; and death and hell wind up the fearful escort. Young men, let the temperance banner wave over you! Be its unflinching advocates, be its fast friends. Never traffic in ardent spirits; and rather die than " deal out death by the half-pint." Oh, what a meeting will there be between the rum-seller and his victim in the resurrection morn!

Young men, you must exert a great influence in your day and generation, for good or evil. Remember there are two great interests set up on earth, and they are antagonistical. Oh, see to it, that the full weight of your influence be on the right side. Be bold in your opposition to every-thing that is evil, and demoralizing; be valiant for the truth; " Serve the God of your fathers with a perfect heart, and with a willing mind." Tell me not, that zeal in the cause of virtue, of religion, and of God, will interfere with your other engagements or lawful callings in life. By no means will it. You may have the plough, or the pen in your hand, and God in your heart at the same time. In every calling, in every profession, in every pursuit of life, you may find illustrations of the fact, that piety and the lawful pursuits of life, are by no means incompatible with each other.

Do you wish to be a lawyer? Be it so. Selden was a lawyer, and Selden was a very pious man. Do you covet the office of a judge? Very well. Sir Matthew Hale was a judge, and Sir Matthew Hale was a most devoted Christian. Do you desire to be a physician? Be it so. Boerhaave was a physician, and no one questions his piety. Would you be a merchant? Bethune was a merchant, and so was Robert Ralston, and who knows not that their praise is in all the churches? But you must be a mechanic. Be it so ; that is an honourable calling; Harlan Page was a mechanic, and Harlan Page had many, converted by his instrumentality, to rise up and call him blessed.

The apostle says, " Whatsoever you do, do it heartily as unto the Lord." The idea is this, that *duties never clash.* You can be a zealous, warm-hearted Christian, and at the same time be active and enterprising in all the lawful callings and pursuits of life. Indeed, he who professes to be a Christian, and neglects his temporal duties, dishonours the name of Christ; hence the language of the apostle, "He that provides not for his own, especially for those of his own household, hath denied the faith, and is worse than an infidel;" and the rule laid down, which embraces all duties, whether of a temporal or spiritual nature, is this : "Whatsoever thy hand findeth to do, do it with thy might, for there is no work, nor device, nor knowledge, nor wisdom, in the grave, whither thou goest." Yes, in relation to everything which claims your attention, be active and diligent, remembering the words of our blessed Redeemer, "The night cometh when no man can work." But, as we have said, our text embraces,

II. Considerations which are worthy of the attention of all, but particularly of young men.

The first is expressed in these words : "The Lord searcheth all hearts, and understandeth all the imaginations of the thoughts." The idea is this, that the eye of God is upon you; that He knows not only all your actions, but all your thoughts. He is with you at all times, by night and by day, at home and abroad, and is perfectly acquainted with your whole character; you are ever in his immediate presence, and have to say, with Hagar in the wilderness, "Thou, God, seest me!" What a powerful consideration this is to hold the sinner in check, and make him anxious neither to do, or say, or think, anything that is wrong. "Thou, God, seest me!" The bare thought of it is enough to make the dagger to fall from the hand of the assassin. The bare thought of it is enough to cause the cup to fall from the hand of the inebriate; and enough also, to cause the oath to die half uttered upon the tongue. Oh, remember, young man, that you can hide nothing from your Maker, that every sin you commit is known and registered, and that the day of review must come!

The second consideration is this : "If thou seek Him, He will be found of thee." Oh, if you only knew what is implied in finding God ; if you only knew how rich and happy this would make you ! Count up all the silver and the gold in this wide world ; add every diamond and every pearl ; add all the kingdoms on earth, and the glory of them, and what is all this to the favour of God ! The favour of God!—it is everything which men on earth, or angels in heaven can desire ; hence the language of the Psalmist: "Thy favour, O God, is life ; Thy loving-kindness is better than life." This is the prize presented, and how is it to be obtained ? By seeking. "If thou seek Him, He will be found of thee." If some one, in whom you have confidence, should tell you that there is a jewel hid in the sand near your dwelling, which is worth one hundred thousand dollars, and that if you seek it you shall find it, and finding it, it shall be yours, would you not seek it? Ay, would you not immediately enter upon the work of seeking it? Would you not seek it by sun-light and star-light—by moon-light and torch-light? and would you not seek it with all your heart— with unwearied perseverance, and with a settled determination never to give over, but to seek until you should find it? Now, this is the promise made, this is the assurance given in relation to the one Pearl of great price. "If thou seek Him, He will be found of thee." And now, if you wish to find the eternal God, as the rest and portion of your soul; if you wish to repose in his bosom, and share in his everlasting love, you must seek Him as directed—"Seek ye the Lord while He may be found, and call upon Him while He is near."

But in this matter there are certain things which must not be forgotten: 1. You are to seek the Lord while you are yet in the morning of life. Few persons, comparatively speaking, are converted after they are thirty years of age. The season of youth, ah! that is the golden season, the best season; hence this special command given, "Remember now thy Creator in the days of thy youth;" and, also, this special promise, which we find upon sacred record, "They that seek Me early shall find Me."

2. You are to seek the Lord in the forsaking of all your sins, as it is written, "Let the wicked forsake his way, and the unrighteous man his thoughts; let him return unto the Lord, and He will have mercy upon him; and to our God, for He will abundantly pardon." Yes, this is a settled point; you are to give up all your sins, even your most loved and besetting sin. Though dear as a right hand, you must cut it off : though dear as a right eye, you must pluck it out. The sacrifice may be esteemed great, but it must be made, for the Psalmist says, "If I regard iniquity in my heart, the Lord will not hear me;" and if you indulge in one single sin, even in your heart, why should He hear you ? Remember, you cannot be earthly-minded and heavenly-minded at the same time. "You cannot serve God and Mammon."

This leads me to make a third remark : You must seek the Lord earnestly; you must seek Him with all your heart, even as the hungry man seeks bread, the thirsty man seeks water, or as the ambitious man seeks fame. Your whole soul must be in the matter. You must feel that everything that is dear is at stake—that, if you succeed, you are happy for ever; if you succeed not, you are undone to all eternity. Oh, then, let this be with you the great concern, to seek and find God, as your supreme good and the portion of your soul. And for your encouragement, remember it is written, " Then shall ye seek Me, and find Me, when you search for Me with all your heart." Take God at his word. Believe the promise, and your salvation is sure. Your sins will be pardoned; God will be your Father, and heaven your sweet and everlasting home !

But a third consideration or motive, presented in our text, is expressed in these emphatic words, " But if thou forsake Him, He will cast thee off for ever." Here we have, as it were, the mutterings of the thunders of the last day. The language is awful : how does it fall upon your ear ? Listen ! " But, if thou forsake Him, He will cast thee off for ever." My young friends, suppose your parents' should cast you off; suppose your brothers and sisters should cast you off; suppose your friends and neighbours—suppose the whole world should cast you off, would you not esteem yourselves wretched ? Let my father and my mother cast me off; let my brothers and my sisters cast me off; let my friends and my neighbours—let all the world cast me off, but, O God of my salvation, do not thou cast me off ! for, if driven from thy presence, whither, oh whither shall I go ?

Permit me to remark, that, when I was

quite a youth, one of Watts' hymns made a very deep and lasting impression upon my mind, particularly these lines :—

> " That awful day will surely come,
>   The appointed hour makes haste,
> When I must stand before my Judge,
>   And pass the solemn test.

> " Thou lovely Chief of all my joys,
>   Thou Sovereign of my heart,
> How could I bear to hear thy voice
>   Pronounce the word, DEPART.

> " The thunder of that dismal word
>   Would so torment my ear,
> 'Twould tear my soul asunder, Lord,
>   With most tormenting fear.

> " What ! to be banished from my life,
>   And yet forbid to die ?
> To linger in eternal pain,
>   And death for ever fly ?"

These lines came over my soul with a most awakening influence—with a most tremendous power; but the following verse crowned the whole :—

> " Oh ! wretched state of deep despair,
>   To see my God remove,
> And fix my doleful station, where
>   I must not taste his love !"

The scenes of the last great day were brought vividly before the eyes of my mind. There was the Judge enthroned—there the vast multitude of the human family assembled—the righteous on the right hand, the wicked on the left; and a great gulf between. Amongst the happy ones, I pictured to myself many of my dearest relatives, and, above all, my sainted mother! The Judge smiled upon them, but there was no smile for me. I must depart! Cut off from God, and his angels, and all whom I loved on earth, I must take an everlasting farewell. Driven away, I must wander down the vale of an unblest eternity—a wretched, hopeless exile from God, and happiness, and heaven. Oh, ye dear youth, who have been blessed with pious parents, and who have been early taught the great truths of our holy religion, how could you bear to see your "God remove"? How can you endure the thought of having your doleful station fixed where you "must not taste his love"? Never, no, never, never more! Oh, eternity! eternity! To be exiled from God, and happiness, and heaven for a million of years—how overwhelming the thought! But, oh, for ever! "Who can paraphrase" (as a poor dying sinner said), "who can paraphrase upon the words, for ever and for ever?" My young friends, remember, great eternity is before you, and what you now do this night may stamp your character, and fix your destiny for ever! You may try to hide these things from your eyes; you may try to forget them altogether, but this will avail nothing.

God has appointed a day wherein He will judge the world; yea, even the secrets of all hearts. Amid the scenes of youth, and the pursuits and pleasures of this life, you may perhaps enjoy yourselves, and get along without God and religion; but what will you do when the evil days shall come, and the years draw nigh, when you shall say, I have no pleasure in them. In the morning of life, when everything is smiling around you, it is quite possible that you may have something like joy playing around your heart; but what will you do in the day when the sun, and the light, and the moon, are darkened, and the clouds return after the rain? You may get along without God, it may be, when you are yet young, and everything is smiling upon you; but what will you do when the keepers of the house shall tremble, and the strong men shall bow themselves, and the grinders shall cease because they are few, and those that look out of the windows are darkened? You may get along without God, it may be, when you are yet young, and everything is smiling around you; but what will you do in the day when you shall be afraid of that which is high; and fears shall be in the way, and the almond-tree shall flourish, and [the grasshopper shall be a burden, and desire shall fail, because man goeth to his long home, and the mourners go about the streets? You may get along without God and

religion, perchance, while you are yet young, and
everything is smiling around you ; but what will
you do in the day when the silver cord shall be
loosed, and the golden bowl shall be broken; in
the day when the pitcher shall be broken at the
fountain, and the wheel broken at the cistern ; in
the day when the dust shall return to the earth as
it was, and the spirit shall return unto God who
gave it ?

Young men, listen to me : this world has a
powerful charm for many, and especially for the
young; the influence which it exerts over multitudes is truly astonishing; and, after all, what is
the world, but a " land of unsubstantial shades ? "
and what are the things of the world, but an
empty, though brilliant show ?   So teaches Solomon—" Vanity of vanities," says he, " all is
vanity."   Observe, this is not the language of a
poverty-stricken man, who, under the influence of
envious feelings, cries down those things which he
possesses not.   Nor is it the longing of a carping
cynic, who, soured by disappointment, would retire
from the world in disgust.   No ; nor is it the language of a man who utters in a moment of excitement that which he would fain recall in the
season of calm reflection.   It is the language of a
man famed for his riches, and wisdom, and prosperity.   It is the language of Solomon, the son of
David, the king of Israel.   No man, probably,

that ever lived, was better qualified to form a correct estimate of the world and the things of the world, for, it seems, there was no source of worldly enjoyment to which he had not repaired in his pursuit after happiness, and here he gives the result of his long-continued observation, the verdict of his own dear-bought experience—"Vanity of vanities, all is vanity." Notice, Solomon does not affirm that some earthly things are vain, but all— "Vanity of vanities, all is vanity." Not that Solomon intended to say that, literally, there is nothing good or desirable on earth. His idea is this: as the supreme good, or portion of the soul, everything of an earthly nature is weighed and found wanting. This falls in with the language of the poet:—

"The world can never give,
The bliss for which we sigh."

And, if I mistake not, this falls in also with the experience of the gayest of the gay, now present. Ah! believe me, "There is nothing true, there is nothing firm, there is nothing sweet but heaven!" Oh, my young friends, in view of all these things, be persuaded to seek something better than this world can give. The world! how vain will it appear when you are sinking in the cold embrace of death! The world! what a poor thing, what a beggarly portion, when it shall be wrapped in the winding-sheet of the last great conflagration: and oh! how utterly unworthy of the aspirations of an immortal mind, must all its riches, and honours, and splendours this moment appear to those bright spirits who are now high in the climes of bliss, and bathing in glory, as in the sunlight of heaven! Therefore, young men, listen, oh listen. I again entreat you, to consider the language of the text; it was the dying charge of a father to a son whom he loved; and it may in substance be the charge given to some of you by some beloved parent now gone to glory. Oh hear it, as the counsel of experience and love! Oh receive, it as the voice of an oracle, or angel of God :—" My son, know thou the God of thy father, and serve Him with a perfect heart, and with a willing mind : for the Lord searcheth all hearts, and understandeth all the imaginations of the thoughts. If thou seek Him, He will be found of thee; but if thou forsake Him He will cast thee off for ever."

The End.

Other Titles for Young Men

In addition to *Addresses to Young Men* you are holding in your hands we are happy to offer the following related titles to help equip you to war the good warfare of our Lord:

Assurance of Faith by Louis Berkhof

The Backslider: *Nature, Symptoms & Recovery* by Andrew Fuller

My Brother's Keeper: *Letters to a Younger Brother* by J.W. Alexander

The Chief End of Man by John Hall

Church Member's Guide by John Angell James

Come Ye Apart: *Gospel Devotions* by J.R. Miller

Communicant's Companion by Matthew Henry

Divine Love: *Sermons on the Love of the Triune God* by John Eadie

Friendship: *The Master Passion* by H. Clay Trumbull

Imago Christi: *The Example of Jesus Christ* by James Stalker

Jesus of Nazareth: *Character, Teaching & Miracles* by J.A. Broadus

The Man of Business by J.W. Alexander, W.B. Sprague and more

Manual for the Young by Charles Bridges

Notes on Galatians by J. Gresham Machen

Opening Scripture: *Hermeneutical Manual* by Patrick Fairbairn

Opening Up Ephesians by Peter Jeffery

Pastor's Sketches: *Case Studies with Troubled Souls* by I.S. Spencer

Pathway into the Psalter by William Binnie

Paul the Missionary by Louis Berkhof

Paul the Preacher: *Studies on Discourses in Acts* by John Eadie

Power of God unto Salvation by Benjamin B. Warfield

Secret of Communion with God by Matthew Henry

The Still Hour: *Communion with God in Prayer* by Austin Phelps

The Transfigured Life: *Selected Shorter Writings of J.R. Miller*

The Travels of True Godliness: *An Allegory* by Benjamin Keach

Whatsoever Things are True: *Discourses on Truth* by J.H. Thornwell

The Word & Prayer: *Devotions from Minor Prophets* by John Calvin

Call us Toll Free at 1-877-666-9469
Send us an e-mail at sgcb@charter.net
Visit us on line at solid-ground-books.com

Printed in the United States
71115LV00001B/115-174